PEA SOUP

(WITH A LITTLE HAM ADDED)

JAMES DAILY

To Irene
another struggling
author. Good luck
Jim

This book is dedicated to all those wonderful senior citizens who have survived childhood, wars, working and parenthood.

Acknowledgements

My thanks to my wonderful wife Linda who has brought happiness into my life again.

To my children Kathy, Dave, Steve, Debbie, Sandy, Jim, Chad and Tamara.

To my grandchildren Ben, Josh, Katie, Andrea, Jake, Thuy Thi, Will, Kelly, Zack, Desiree, Cassandra, Mitchell, Sarah, Kayla and Zharia.

To Julia and Jim, Jill, Erik and Spencer.

To my many friends and all those wonderful campers who have come into my life.

A special thanks to Al Kant who graciously gave me a new computer and started me on this journey.

CONGRATULATIONS

Congratulations to all you people who are retired and to those who are close to retiring. This book is especially for you. I am 75, retired, and I want to share with you how successful and enjoyable my retirement years are going.

If you're retired, are you bored? Do you have too much time on your hands? Are you wondering how it will be? You've waited all this time and you really want it to be the "GOLDEN YEARS". Rest assured that this can be a very rewarding time in your life. I will share with you how my life has been filled with happiness even after tragedy. Great expectations can come true if you guide your life in the right direction. It worked for me.

In my book I take you down the memorable path to yesterday that you all will enjoy. My story could well be your story.

This book has poetry, humor, stories of my foster girls that will tug at your heartstrings and a love story to boot. It even has something for the spiritual who have God in their lives. I tried to show you how to leave a legacy. I think you will find my book enjoyable and humorous.

God bless you all,
James Daily

CHAPTER 1

VOLUNTEER WORK

The first thing I suggest is to do some kind of volunteer work. Remember, we have a lot more time on our hands than people who are working. God knows every community needs volunteers. It can be very rewarding. You didn't really want to sit around all day and read or watch TV, did you? Of course not. Many organizations out there are just crying for people with your skills.

I'll even put in a plug for Big Brothers and Big Sisters, which is a great organization. You can be a mentor for some child. I was a Big for a few years and enjoyed it very much. You can open a whole new world for them and make a small friend in the process.

I was also a CASA worker, which means Court Appointed Special Advocate. You become a voice for a kid in court. It is much like being a social worker. I was assigned to a special case and worked in conjunction with Social Services. I had to undergo 30 hours of training, but it was interesting and I met some new friends.

It is a program that has a hard time getting volunteers because it is time consuming, but seniors have all kinds of time. You have to attend court, make home visits along with visitations to foster homes and attend meetings.

Another program that I am still active in and have been for over 20 years is teaching religious education to physically and mentally challenged people. They need teachers badly. This program is very rewarding because I have found those I teach needy and friendly. They appreciate everything I do for them. We put on plays that they participate in. There is singing and we teach them about God. You don't really need any special training; just be yourself. The work you do will make you realize how lucky you are.

I'd like to share one incident that has been taking place for the past several weeks. There is a young girl who has Downs Syndrome who is in our Saturday program. She came up to me and said, that she always prays for me. How's that for making you feel humble?

This really touched my heart. It gave me an idea of how beautiful these special people are. Every Thanksgiving a great organization called "The Northside Improvement League" puts on a beautiful dinner for all of them. At the end of the year, around May, we have a nice picnic with hamburgers and hot dogs for them. It is really a fun program.

COUNSELING AT A SUMMER CAMP

To counsel for a week in the summer at a church camp is a great joy. If you want to feel young again, then by all means look up your local church and find out where the programs are in your area.

It is so rewarding to be out in the woods so close to God and to be with wonderful young people. I do devotions and counseling at a real beautiful camp in the Adirondacks. They have a slogan, "Where lives are changed." Believe me, it happens. We sleep in cabins and spend a joy-filled week. We have pizza night and talent night (where I make a fool of myself), volleyball games, and we even get to make homemade ice cream with everyone helping. Does it sounds like fun? It certainly is.

I'd like to tell you about a funny incident that happened a year ago. I was doing morning devotions in an outdoor church in the woods that has logs for seats and a real stone pulpit. Well, I was half way through my talk on this beautiful morning when all of a sudden I heard hoof beats close by. The next thing I knew, three deer ran right toward us with the biggest one just brushing by me heading for the center of the church. He stumbled in the aisle, got back up and scampered by two girls sitting in the back. When the dust cleared, we found that one of the boys had been struck slightly on the side of the head by a hoof. He was okay after being examined by a nurse. The funny part was when she asked him what happened, he said that he had been kicked by a deer. After that incident we called him Deer Slayer and he was the butt of a few good-natured jokes that he took with a grin. He had a great story to tell his parents and the kids at school when he got home.

Even when camp ends everyone keeps in touch via email. Our camp is called, "Friends." We also formed an on line prayer circle for anyone who needs prayer. We are a close bunch. It's worth trying.

I remember reading in the Bible when the disciples wanted to keep the young children away from Jesus, He said, "Let the little children come unto Me for such is the kingdom of heaven." He loved kids, can I not do the same?

I have become a pen pal to all my campers making sure I email them often during the year or even write letters sometimes. I always send them Christmas cards. Sometimes it amazes the kids that I never forget them. Even for some of them who were only at camp a few years ago, I still try to keep in contact with them.

They tell me how college is going and what is happening in general in their life. I care because once I make a friend, I don't want to lose them.

One of the young counselors was married last summer, and I went to her wedding. She was a former camper and now lives in Norway but we always keep in touch via email. Love travels across the ocean. She is expecting a little girl and tells me about Norway.

It always amazes me that we can keep in touch so many miles away. It is like she is in my living room. Love is at the tip of my fingers on the keyboard.

Another camper whom I haven't heard from in two years, suddenly wrote to me from Italy where she was visiting. They never seem to forget the times at camp.

One girl who is too old for camp wrote me recently and told me she never attended church until she went to camp. She confided in me that after hearing my devotions, she and her mother go to church.

Volunteer work can be very rewarding.

CHAPTER 2

OWN A PET

I have had pets at various stages in my life, but I find the ideal time to have one is after you retire. You have more time to spend with them, more time to enjoy them. They say pets have a calming effect on you and that they are good for your blood pressure. I do know that a dog or cat can give you a feeling of peace. Cats lay on your lap and are quiet and dogs are very loyal, wanting to be near you and lay at your feet.

About a year ago, we acquired two Siamese cats, a brother and sister and they have brought us much joy. They are very intelligent and loveable. To think at one time I thought this breed was mean. How wrong I was.

We also have a greyhound dog that my wife rescued. She once raced.   Tina is a gentle animal, never paying any attention to the cats.

Just a short time ago, there was a stray cat, part Siamese, on our front porch every morning, so we now have three cats. We adopted him, and he fits in great with the others. We had to call him Buster because he is twice the size of the other cats.

It is a joy to watch the cats play together and nap together. Our dog loves to ride in the van with us and be near us. They all sleep in our room at night. There is a certain contentment that comes with having a pet. They are a lot of company especially if you live alone.

CHAPTER 3

KNOW YOURSELF

When you look in the mirror, do you like what you see? I don't mean how you look outside, but go deeper below the surface.

Remember it is never too late to change. If you're not satisfied with yourself, do something about it. There's an old saying that if you're on your knees you will never stumble. Talk to the Man upstairs a lot now that you have time to spare. He's probably been waiting a long time to have a heart to heart talk with you.

Don't take yourself too seriously. Smile a lot; it puts wonderful laugh lines on your face (they are the best kind).

Remember that you don't get respect because you are old you get it because you earned it.

Don't worry that you have more time behind you then ahead of you, use that precious time more wisely. In His service.

Don't worry about the stairs being too hard to climb, thank God that you can still climb them.

When people ask how old you are, tell them that you were a waiter at the Last Supper, or that you're older than snow.

Joke a lot…by now those old jokes will be new to most people.

Take time to listen to someone's problems. There's an old saying, "Laugh and the world laughs with you, cry and you cry alone." Change this and cry along with them. It will cleanse your soul.

One of my campers wrote me a short while ago and told me her little brother who is in first grade has a rare disease of the hip and sockets. He will need several operations and always walk with a limp.
When I read this, tears rolled down my face.

Showing your feelings doesn't mean you're old and senile, it means you're getting closer to God.

My favorite passage in the Bible is when Jesus was at the funeral of Lazareth, and it said, "Jesus wept."

CHAPTER 4

HOBBIES

Get a hobby. There are so many out there. If you can draw but never had the time, or paint, do it now. My daughter is a wonderful artist but she has little time because she works all day. I am sure when she retires that she will do this full time.

I love to dabble in poetry, and I will share some with you later on in this book. I think poets put their true feelings on paper. I love to exchange poems with my friends because I can almost look into the eyes of their soul in their writings.

Write a story about your life like I am doing so your kids or grand kids will have something to remember you by. Make a journal about your feelings. It will mean a lot to people who love you. Remember, you are very important to them and they will treasure anything you have to say. Especially after you've gone it will mean even more to them.

Go fishing. It doesn't matter if the fish are biting or not, just take time to relax and enjoy God's creation. If you're going to be a fisherman, then remember fisherman tell a lot of stories.

Each time they tell the story of the one that got away, they increase the size a little.

I'd like to tell you a story I read of a man who had retired and lived in Florida. He wasn't rich, but his income left him comfortable. There were some people in the vicinity who were poor. The man loved to buy bags of groceries and sneak up on their porches at night and leave them there to find in the morning. His hobby was making people feel good. Remind you of Santa Claus? His wife knew he did this but she didn't care because she saw how happy he was afterwards.

My son knew a young woman who had a nine-year old daughter and who worked hard making ends meet. Around Christmas time we put together a food basket with meat and canned goods, enough for dinner and then some. We bought some gifts for her daughter, too. I can't remember when I felt so good. It is truly more blessed to give than receive.

One time my grandson and I were getting off Route 81 after having breakfast at my favorite truck stop and there was a man with a sign that said, “Will work for food.” I reached in my pocket while we were at the stop sign and found a loose $10 bill and handed it to my grandson to give to the man. He took the money and waved to me with a big smile on his face.

Now I know you are going to say that he conned me and would spend the money on booze. Well, we went shopping for a while and when we were driving home, I saw the same man eating a big sandwich, so I do know he spent some of the money on food. It showed my grandson it’s nice to share.

Getting back to hobbies, you might want to take rides in the country and take some pictures of nature. Walk down a winding dirt road because dirt roads are nostalgic.

Get a bird book and see if you can recognize the different species. Commune with nature.

If you are musically inclined, you are never too old to take lessons. After all these years, my son is starting to play the piano again and we gave him lessons when he was a little boy.

If you like playing cards, have a card night in your house or find a group that plays on different nights. It tests your brain and is really very enjoyable. You make new friends.

If you like to bowl you can join a league

or go bowling with some of your friends. You can have a nice night out and just maybe meet some new people. It's nice to get out of the house.

Near Albany where my daughter lives, there is an older couple that have no children who are her neighbors. They often take my daughters two boys on trips to Vermont or to dinner. The boys really love this couple. It is so very rewarding hanging out with young people. They are honest and tell it like it is. I like that. My email address book is full of young people who write me all the time. Age is certainly no barrier unless you make it one.

Hobbies come in all sizes. Pick one that fits.

CHAPTER 5

WHY I LOVE MY COMPUTER

I just love my computer, if it's possible to love something that isn't flesh and blood. My email address book is overflowing with my many friends, young and old alike. I don't need any stamps or wait for the snail mail to get to my friends. I just write my letter and push send, and away it goes. A lot of you seniors are going to say you're too old to learn how to use one but you're not. I never took up typing but get along great using one finger on the keyboards. Of course, when my grandkids see me do this, they get a big laugh but I get the job done.

The story I am going to tell about my computer will have a special interest to all you widows and widowers out there. I know it's lonely because I have been there. Let me tell you my story.

I was once married to the most beautiful woman on the face of the earth. For 48 years it was a marriage made in heaven that produced six children plus two adopted ones. I had a wonderful job I loved, and a beautiful family to match. No man could have asked for anything more. Then one day my wife was diagnosed with breast cancer and the world fell on me. When she passed away, I no longer wanted to live. I was even angry at God. Only those of you who have lost someone you loved dearly can begin to know how I felt.

About three years later, I was given a computer by a good friend of my son's. I think he knew in his heart that this was what I needed. At first I just used it for copying my poems and saving them.

Now I am the type who needs someone to hold and hug.

Sometimes I felt guilty because I loved my wife so very much, but she was gone and I was still here.

I was 72 and thought, who would want me now? I'm way past my prime, what do I have to offer anyone? Then I looked in the mirror, looked deep into the real me and decided that I have a lot to offer a woman even at my age.

I was a good husband and father, never drank or smoked and had good habits. I cared for people and loved my God (after we had reconciled, and I no longer blamed Him for my tragedy).

I knew some others around my age who had remarried, but I thought that that wasn't for me either. I did notice that the ones who had stayed single seemed unhappy, and I thought I knew why.

One very good friend who had lost her husband went for coffee one night with me and we shared a lot. Before I dropped her home, she started crying and I put my arms around her for comfort. She seemed to need that and I tried to tell her that she should try to find someone.

Well, one night when I was playing with my computer, I got an email to join a singles site. All I had to do was answer some questions, choose a fictitious name and type in what I was looking for in a woman. After completing this, I sat back and waited, checking my email every day to see if anything was happening. To my surprise, some women started writing me at this site. I gave them my real email address and the fun began.

There were lonely women out there who were looking for a companion. Well, I traveled to Syracuse twice to see different women and once to Oswego, but nothing happened. There wasn't any chemistry. Then, one woman and I started writing. and she told me I was too old for her, so I asked if she would like to be a pen pal, and we seemed to hit it off. She worked at a school about 100 miles away and we emailed a couple times a day. She began to confide in me and told me personal things she said she never told anyone else. We even talked about our dates we had. I was glad at the time she never found anyone serious and she seemed to feel the same way, but our age difference was always there, she was 15 years younger than me.

Then one day, I met a woman online who lived in the Adirondacks. She played guitar and wrote poems like me. We decided to meet on a September day at a halfway mark. We went by a waterfall and talked all afternoon (Well, actually, we did more than talk).

It was the first time I kissed a woman who wasn't my wife. We both had a real nice day and promised to meet again.

But it was never to be.

It seems afterwards she met a fellow she had known before who lived near her and they started dating again. We did part friends, and actually I was a little relieved.

One day my friend who lived 100 miles away invited me to visit her and since she lived in Cooperstown, I brought my two grandkids with me so they could see the Hall of Fame. I think my friend was relieved when she heard my grandkids were coming, maybe she was afraid to be alone with me, we had not met yet. We had a nice weekend and we stayed at her house over night. Nothing happened, not even a kiss. I knew there was that age difference but in a way I was a little disappointed. She did respond to the good-bye hug I gave her.

I even made a train trip to NYC one time but that was a disaster. She wanted me to forget my family and live in with her.

I became discouraged to say the least. The only letters I got were from my friend in Cooperstown and a nice lady from Rome who had been writing me for a long time but never suggested anything romantic. Now I had two nice friends but no romantic interests. Hold on, the plot thickens. I got a letter from a woman that suggested I meet her and her two sisters and I could take my pick. I laughed all the way upstairs.

My hopes were real low when something happened, God intervening you might say. Of course I always felt God was leading me in the right direction. One night when I was about ready to go to bed, I decided to try the state of Pennsylvania and see what happened.

I found one woman who had stated she was "sensuous". I liked that word and decided to write her. Then I went to bed.

The next morning I checked my email and the woman had not only answered my letter but had left her phone number. I dialed her and immediately liked her voice. I found out her name was Linda. That night we talked until dawn broke. She invited me to visit her near the Pocono Mts.

It was a beautiful day that Monday morning when I headed out with much anticipation. I asked God if He could make my heart at ease and hoped I was doing the right thing. The last exit I got off was called, "Lord's Valley" and I thought, "hmm." Then I passed a campground that said, "The Promised Land." He was leading me down a garden path. I was on a road winding through the woods, saw a few deer and began to feel at peace. As I turned on the last road I removed my glasses.

Remember, all of you, if it's been a long time, you kiss better without your glasses on. They really get in the way to kiss especially if she wears glasses too.

I had told Linda that when we met I was going to give her a hug and a gentle kiss. It is nice to give her a warning so she knows what to expect. It's different now that you are older.

Her house was the last one on the left and as I drove closer, I had butterflies in my stomach (don't worry, this is sometimes a normal feeling).

There she was waiting out front for me with a pretty white blouse on and blue jeans and I felt better when I saw her nice smile. I got out of my van and pretended my ankles didn't hurt as I made my way toward her. I gave her a big hug (I always give big hugs), and then cupped her face and gave her my very best gentle kiss. She seemed to like that and when we were done (after a short time of course), she took my hand in hers and led me into her house. I had charmed her.

From the first moment I entered her house I felt very comfortable. It was well kept and she had two beautiful greyhound dogs she had rescued from the track (unfortunately the one dog had to be put away later on).

She had some champagne opened and cheese and crackers on the stand by the couch. Well, I felt like a teen-ager again and we spent a glorious afternoon eating and drinking (I never drink alcoholic beverages, but the champagne was bubbly). We did kiss a lot.

She said she had a guest room for me to stay overnight so I wouldn't have to make the trip in one day. It was a four hour drive.

I visited her on Monday and left on Friday, four days longer than I planned on staying. We had fallen in love in a week's time. The chemistry was very strong. You just know when it happens.

I didn't want to leave, but I had things to take care of. She had packed me a lunch, and when I stopped in a rest area to eat it, there was a note saying she loved me. It was really getting serious.

I arrived home and sent an email to my friend in Cooperstown (the one who said I was too old for her). I told her about Linda and that we were serious and thought she would be happy for me. I was wrong.

She was furious and told me there was still time to change my mind and that she loved me. Well, I found out how little I knew about women, and was about to get a lesson.

I wrote her back and told her she never said there was something romantic going on between us.

I went to bed that night feeling very confused.

My other friend in Rome, who I was going to take to dinner before I met Linda, was very happy for me, and to this day she remains one of my very best friends. I thought I knew women!

My friend in Cooperstown told me she was devastated and that she would never date again.

The next day my phone rang and it was her and I remembered she had never called me at my house. She cried and made me feel like a heel. She asked me if I could visit her one more time and just hold her. I told her I didn't think that would be fair to Linda. I did feel bad because I had lost a friend and I don't like to lose friends.

After that, I visited Linda several more times and brought her to my house to meet my family. Actually, the first time she met them was at my son's birthday party. Everyone liked her a lot. Linda is kind and compassionate and lives up to the word "sensuous."

Three months after we met we were married, two days after my birthday, Christmas. We were married by a Justice of the Peace near her home in Milford, Pa. Linda's niece, Jill and her two sons Erik and Spencer attended. My little granddaughter, Desiree and Spencer were ring bearers. We had a great dinner at a place called Mt. Haven and spent some of the evening at the chalet her niece had rented.

It seemed like a whirlwind romance, but at our age we both knew what we wanted. Time waits for no one.

Next came the problem of selling our houses and finding a new one but everything seemed to fall into place. We now reside in a dream house, a log cabin near the woods in a secluded area, peaceful and content. BUT, the Lord put ideas into our head, saying He wasn't ready for us to settle down on our butt and do nothing but watch the grass grow. He still wanted us to give of ourselves being He had been so good to us. We decided to be foster parents, even at our advanced age, (my advanced age anyway, as I am 12 years older than my wife).

This is where God works in mysterious ways. After we were married, I got Linda to join our handicapped program, so we are still doing some volunteer work.

We thought that maybe we could take in a child around 11 or 12 with hopes of adopting.

CHAPTER 6

KIDS NEEDING LOVE

On this subject, you might just want to look into giving one of God's little ones a nice home with you. You just give them love and get a lot more back in return.

Let me tell you a story of our first year as foster parents. We had been approved by Social Services and didn't even have to put the hours in training because of my work in the CASA program. So we waited in anticipation of who our first child would be. It wasn't as we had planned, as I said before, we wanted to adopt a younger child.

Well, we got a call from Social Service that they needed a home for a 17 year old girl. Valissa was not a happy camper, as she had been in three other foster homes and she was taking a pill for depression. I thought she was very young to be on pills. My wife said she hoped we didn't get any problem kids, and I told her they were all problem kids or they wouldn't be in foster care.

I figured that I had lots of experience because I had 8 kids of my own and had worked around kids all my life.

It turned out that Linda made an excellent foster mother.

I found it a challenge to say the least to try to get through to our new foster girl. Valissa was very shy and laid back and wasn't used to showing her feelings. We have certain rules of the house that we laid out for her (mostly this was Linda's territory). I took care of the long talks when things didn't always go right. Valissa and I formed a bond, a bond of truth, and to this day she has never lied to us. She has a steady boyfriend, a car, a part time job and is doing great in school. I like to think we contributed to her being a normal, well-adjusted teen. She is no longer on depression pills and seems to be leading a happy life.

About four months after we got her, we had a message on our answering machine saying they needed a place for a 17 year-old girl to stay a few days until they could find a foster home for her. LeAnne was a pretty, bubbly girl who seemed to welcome the hug I gave her. She had known Valissa from another foster home and that night she asked if she could stay with us. I am an old softie and I felt sorry for her, so I said yes. The next day I called Social Service and arranged it.

I found out a few days later that LeAnne had been in about 12 foster homes and a place called, "Kids Peace" where they helped problem children. They said she was emotionally disturbed. Le Anne was like taming a wild stallion, and her therapist begged us not to give up on her. We had no intention of doing this. Sure, there were some bad arguments and things were not always rosy, but we stuck in the saddle and rode it through. I think I put that a nice way. It was like breaking a wild stallion. The plan was for her to go home and after six months Social Service agreed to let her go back to her mom, and we were happy for her.

She is a hugger and very affectionate. We knew we were going to miss her. She always called Linda, mom, and me, papa. Kids have a way of growing on you after they have been with you awhile.

After two days of being home, Le called one night on the phone and wanted to come back. Linda told her to give it more time and see what happened. She agreed. She said she would visit us on weekends.

Awhile after she went home, Social Service called and said they needed a home for a 16 year- old girl who was in a home in N.H. called, "Easter Seals" for troubled kids. She also had been in a few other foster homes.

We agreed and gave her Le's room that we thought would be a guest room. The Lord said no. The one love of her life was her grandmother who had died a few months before this.

So much for us adopting a child of our own which was one of the reasons we got into foster care in the first place. Was God using me? I was to find out sooner than I expected.

The new girl seemed to be happy here, calling us mom and papa and things seemed to be running smoothly. As I get older, I come to the conclusion that life isn't always supposed to run smooth and the sooner we adjust to this fact and go with the flow, the better for us.

LeAnne came to visit one weekend and told us she was very unhappy and wanted to come back. We told her that we had given her room away and she said she would share it. You've heard the old saying, "Never a dull moment." So it has been since Linda and I married.

We couldn't put Le out so we checked with our new foster girl and she said it was fine with her. Christy agreed to share her room.

The girls seemed to be getting along well, singing and listening to music together. Everything was going great we thought!!!

Social Services wanted the new girl, Christy, out of our home because they thought LeAnne was too emotional for her.

They moved Christy to another home and she ran away after three days. She came back to our house crying.

We were at a meeting in the church down the road, so she went to her aunt's place where she now resides. Christy's aunt welcomed her.

After obtaining permission from Le-Anne's mother, Le is still residing with us. We are supporting her as she is no longer a foster child. We love her like our own daughter so God has been good to us and whatever happens next is in His hands.

Many of you will choose not to be foster parents for different reasons, and that is your choice. I remember an old saying that goes like this, "Open your home to strangers for you might be entertaining an angel." I think Le is our angel to whom we opened our door to.

All I'm saying is try to do something on this earth to give back to God what He has done for you. Maybe it's giving someone a ride to the store who has no car. It could be visiting a nursing home and reading to someone whose eyesight is bad. You could invite your next door neighbor who is lonely over to dinner some night.

The options to help people are everywhere. Give something of yourself, your time, your skills, and your talent.

KEEP GIVING

Our time on this earth is limited. You can't use it any more wisely then giving of yourself to help others. There's no better time than after you have retired, when you have nothing but time on your hands to do something nice.

Use your talents. If you are a good cook, then bake some pies or cookies and share them. I remember an old Italian lady who canned chili relish that would melt in your mouth and she would different times give me a quart jar. You could never buy relish like she made.

Have some young neighbors kids help you bake cookies or cup cakes; you will have a ball. Tell them stories about your childhood.

There was an old lady who lived across the street from me and my kids were always in her house listening to the tales she would spin. They truly loved her and to this day have never forgotten her.

Years ago when I peddled papers, there was this nice lady who always gave me cake and ice cream along my route. In my heart I loved her. I cried when she died.

Don't think because you are a senior that you have to hang out with people your age (though this is okay too). I think I have way more young friends than I do older people.

You'll be surprised how much younger people like you and respect you. If you feel young and act that way, you will fit right in with the young crowd. I remember some campers saying that I acted more like a camper than a counselor. I took this as a great compliment.

Sometimes older people get a reputation of being grouchy and a little moody. Don't let them hang this tag on you.

You'd be surprised at how much a smile can make a person's day.

Don't be afraid to give compliments. It will make that person feel good (and you too) but, be honest.

Learn to laugh a lot, even at your own expense.

CHAPTER 7

A friend of mine sent me some wonderful thoughts on my computer that I would like to share with you.

DO YOU REMEMBER WHEN…?

All the girls had ugly gym uniforms?

It took five minutes to warm up the TV?

Nearly everyone's Mom was at home when the kids got home from school?

Nobody owned a purebred dog?

When a quarter was a decent allowance?

You'd reach into a muddy gutter for a penny?

Your Mom wore nylons that came in two pieces?

All your male teachers wore neckties and female teachers had their hair done each day and wore high heels?

You got your windshield cleaned, oil checked, and gas pumped without asking, all for free, every time?

And you didn't pay for air? And you got trading stamps to boot?

Laundry detergent had free glasses, dishes or towels hidden inside the box?

It was considered a great privilege to be taken to dinner at a real restaurant with your parents?

They threatened to keep kids back a grade if they failed…and they did?

When a 57 Chevy was everyone's dream car… to cruise, peel out, lay rubber or watch submarine races, and people went steady?

No one ever asked where the keys were because they were always in the car, in the ignition, and the doors were never locked.

Playing baseball with no adults to help kids with the rules of the game?

Stuff from the store came without safety caps and hermetic seals because no one had yet tried to poison a perfect stranger?

When being sent to the principal's office was nothing compared to the fate that awaited the student at home?

Basically we were in fear for our lives, but it wasn't because of drive-by shootings, drugs, gangs, etc.

Our parents and grandparents were a much bigger threat! But we survived because their love was greater than the threat.

Do you remember Nancy Drew, the Hardy Boys, Laurel and Hardy, Howdy Dowdy and the Peanut Gallery, the Lone Ranger, The Shadow Knows, Nellie Bell, Roy and Dale, Trigger and Buttermilk?

As well as summers filled with bike rides, baseball games, hula hoops, bowling and visits to the pool, and eating Kool-Aid powder with sugar. Didn't that feel good to say, "Yeah, I remember that?"

CHAPTER 8

WHEN I WAS A BOY

Just thought I would take you on a little trip down memory lane. They really were, "The good old days". No matter what people say. I remember rolling tires for fun and playing horseshoes in the back yard.

My dad loved to go fishing but he worked six days a week and his only day off was Sunday. We would pack a lunch with my mom's homemade bread, put the big German shepherd in the old Chevy and head for the river. I'm sure God forgave us for fishing on the Sabbath. We fished from early morning to sunset.

It was so much fun catching those big old bullheads and then having my mom cook them.

During the day, we would take a break and pull the boat by a nearby spring and drink the sparkling water. Dad would tell me stories about the Babe and his favorite Yankee, Lou Gehrig.

A boy, his dog, and his dad, fishing on a lazy summer day. Now that was heaven.

My dad sent away for a kit to build your own boat. It came pre-cut, ready to be put together. This turned out to be a neighborhood project, every one lending their expertise. When the boat was finally put together, we painted it red, white and blue. It was the most patriotic boat ever built by human hands. It never leaked a drop either.

I think more snow fell when I was a boy than any time after. We never heard of snow blowers, we just operated snow shovels on boy power. I remember shoveling snow so deep you had to do it in layers. On the coldest days, I would be sweating, but it was a good sweat called manual labor. Now days kids think manual labor is the president of Mexico.

At night when the wind was howling and the snow was falling, I made 100 trips to the cellar to bring up coal to feed the two old stoves we had, one in the kitchen to cook on and a pot belly stove in the living room for heat.

I would stand by it to get warm and the front of me would be cherry red when my butt was freezing. No TV or computers, just an old Stuart Warner radio that was filled with adventures of the Shadow, Tom Mix and Jack Armstrong, the all American boy.

On weekends I could go to the movies and see a double- feature, both westerns, six cartoons, a serial and the world news and previews of coming attractions for 11 cents. My transportation to the movies was walking the railroad track from my house to public square.

There were no McDonalds or Wendy's or any of the fast food places, but there was a White Castle that had hamburgers and smothered onions that you could smell a mile away. They were irresistible. You could never eat just one.

I had a paper route with 96 papers and netted $5 a week when everyone paid me. This was my first encounter with money (and I had to make change in my head). We didn't have cash registers telling you how much to give back. We had to think a little and exercise our brains.

I bought my first bike paying five dollars a week. It cost $18 and it was a Speed King, truly the most reliable chariot a boy ever owned and it was all mine after a few weeks.

It was capitalism at it's best.

We didn't have to buy expensive toys at the stores. After seeing a Robin Hood movie we went out back, cut some small limbs and made our own bows and arrows. They called it ingenuity back then. We took two bolts and one nut, cut the heads off wooden matchsticks and made our own little bombs, so to speak.

But we never hurt anyone. Most of you remember the bean shooters we used, and what about those rough and tough tackle football games we had under the street lights in a grassy field, no gear, just our old clothes which often got ripped to my mother's dismay.

Remember when Pepsi went to 16 oz.? Boy was that good ice cold. My mom used to put in the window whether she wanted 25lbs of ice or 50. What about those winter mornings when the weather pushed the cream through the cap on a quart of milk? Those were the days.

WARS WERE DIFFERENT

I remember the war years, the good and the bad that came from the big war, WWII. We fought this war to keep the enemy from our shores and the ones we loved. There was no choice left to us when the Japanese bombed Pearl Harbor.

I was eleven at the time the war started. There were no protesters that I can remember. Many brave boys volunteered to serve our country, some lied about their ages to join. I remember a young man named Colin Kelly being the first ace to be shot down. There was a slogan, much like the one, "Remember the Alamo." It was, "Remember Pearl Harbor." When people saw our flag flying back then, it gave them a feeling of pride and to this day, I feel a lump in my throat when I see, “Old Glory.”

The sad part of this time was reading the obituary of soldiers that had been neighbors and would no longer be coming home. When the war first started, we seemed to be fighting a loosing battle and I was worried what would happen if we were bombed.

I remember on those balmy summer nights when a siren would pierce the air warning every one to turn their lights off. It was a mock air-raid drill and I thought it was so cool to go outdoors with my friends when it was pitch black. Volunteer air raid wardens would come around to make sure every one turned their lights off.

Gas was rationed and even sugar and meat. Everyone was instructed to tighten their belts.

The war ended as I turned 18 and thank God I missed the fighting and people wouldn’t have to die anymore to be free.

Just another trip down memory lane and it could be named, the good, the bad and the ugly. I think it was mostly good.

CHAPTER 9

LEAVE A LEGACY

I don't know about you, but I hope after I'm gone, someone besides my family will remember me and what I contributed. I'm hoping someone will say, "He made a difference."

We're not going to make a difference by saying, "I'm too old and I hurt all over." Forget it. You're not too old and this is a cop-out. If I offend anyone, I'm sorry but I have to tell it the way I see it.

You might ask, "How do you leave a legacy?" You might say that you were a good husband, a good father, and a good provider. So what, that's what you're supposed to be when you get married. You might also say that you worked all your life and deserve to take it easy now. That might be true, but it's no way to leave a legacy.

You've got to want to be better. Remember that saying when you were a kid, (Good, better best, never let it rest, 'till the good is better and the better is best). If you're better than good but not the best, then you have to keep trying.

I've told you in the previous chapters what you have to do to make a difference. You have to give of your most precious commodity, YOU. You have to give of your time and talents. Volunteer for something worthwhile, maybe dishing out soup for the Salvation Army, visiting the sick, sponsoring some child overseas. Do something. Make a friend, communicate. Use your talent. Get involved in your community, you live there. You have more to offer than you ever dreamed of. The beautiful part is that you will feel better about yourself and people will begin to talk about you in a nice way. You will become more loveable.

When people see you come in a room, your light will start to shine, just like the bible says. You will feel alive and forget how old you are because it won't matter. You'll quit feeling sorry for yourself and start feeling sorry for people less fortunate.

Make your stay here worthwhile. You might even become a legend.

Be a leader, people will look up to you mainly because you have been around longer so use it to your advantage. God has given you years of wisdom; act like you're smart.

Say prayers for those you love and for all your friends, it just might be the best thing you can do for them and don't be afraid to tell them you are praying for them. Don't be ashamed of God, you'll be coming face to face with Him soon enough.

If you're afraid of what is beyond, remember His comforting words, "In My Father's house are many mansions and I go to prepare a place for you." And to confirm this, He said, "If this were not true I wouldn't be telling you it."

I don't know about you, but that's all the encouragement I need. All your good deeds will precede you to Heaven so send a lot of them ahead of you.

I don't mean to turn this book into a bible but knowing He lives in my heart each day sure gives me a lot of peace. I am literally a "King's Kid" because He loves me so much.

More things are wrought by prayer than any other way.

Even in my advanced years, I know nothing is going to happen to me that Him and I can't handle. With Him on my side I am a majority.

I remember a few times when I was asked to play Santa Claus and how rewarding it was to have all those little children sit on my lap and look at me with those adoring eyes filled with love. For a little while I felt like God. Even some of the older ones sat on my lap, trying to be funny, but I think it brought back fond memories to them.

Young people have so much to offer, especially teen-agers. Spend some time talking with them and see how much you will be rewarded. Most teenagers are truthful and don't pull any punches.

I loved to tell them about my friend, Jesus, and how very much He loves them. I told them stories about His life and what kind of a man He was, how He was always doing good things for people and why we should try to be like Him.

Some of us like to serve God in an advisory capacity but that doesn't work. He does just fine on His own.

One of the best times I had was two years ago teaching a confirmation class, mainly because two of my grandchildren were there. Now I know most seniors know the bible pretty well and this also would be a wonderful opportunity to volunteer.

There is a beautiful hymn called, "Here I am, Lord." It is a promise to serve Him if He needs you and believe me, with the way the world is going, He needs us more than ever. Never, never say you are too old. If you ask Him to use you, be careful, for He probably will and then what are you going to do? Tell Him you were only kidding.

I wrote a poem telling Jesus I wanted Him to use me, and you know what? He read the poem and took me up on it.

But He always leads you in the right direction. Being a foster parent is quite an experience. Some of my older friends told me they could never do this and I wonder why.

Is it because they treasure their privacy or because they can only get close to family. I can truthfully say that I have loved all three girls that we have had in foster care, and you know something, it wasn't hard for us to love them.

The most rewarding part was to know we helped make a big difference.

The old saying about not being able to save the world, but just maybe saving one child is a start.

Is it really so hard to go the extra mile for someone who is in need and can't make it alone? There is a cute saying that goes like this, "Friends help lift you up when your wings are too tired to fly."

CHAPTER 10

GIVE OF YOURSELF

I remember the poster when I was a boy, of Uncle Sam with his sleeves rolled up and pointing a finger and saying, "I want you." It meant our country needed volunteers for the Army.

I can picture Jesus in the place of Uncle Sam pointing His finger at us and saying He wants us.

We have some people in our Handicapped program who don't teach but give rides to the people who belong in the program but have no transportation.

I know one senior who is in an electric wheel chair but gives communion to the sick in hospitals and the shut-ins. Most older people in a wheel chair would just want to stay home.

You see there are all kinds of excuses we can use to not being bothered but you do want to leave a legacy don't you? Of course you do.

Just last night, I made a new friend I have never seen before. She had sent something religious to a friend of mine email.

I wrote her and started talking about God and she wrote back, and now I have a new friend to add to my address book. My cup runneth over. Reach out.

She started telling me all about herself after I filled her in on my life. Now, though I just met her, I feel a bond between us like I do with all my other friends. Do you feel a close bond with your friends? You should if they are really your friends.

A woman sent me a beautiful definition of friends, "A true friend is someone who reaches for your hand and touches your heart." Friends listen and care when you have something to share or are hurting. They cry with you when you need compassion. Friends care for you always. They are there when you need them, day or night. They are open for you 24 hours a day 7 days a week. A friend always has a shoulder for you to cry on and a hug to lift you up. They are like a precious pearl in an oyster. Good friends give you a warm feeling when the world seems cold. Friends are there even when you're not very likeable sometimes because they see beyond today and look at you inside.

CHAPTER 11

FEAR OF DEATH

This is a touchy subject to most people, young and old alike. There were quite a few teens at camp this year that were very curious about death. Most people want to avoid this subject because they think it is morbid. Probably a lot of parents didn't want to discuss it, maybe because they had no answers or they wanted to talk about happier things. At any rate some campers in our camp wanted to freely discuss it.

One morning in my devotions, I donated the whole time to talk on this subject and it even carried over to our discussion classes. It was important to them to get answers.

I'm not going into bible verses but I did quote Paul's letter to the Corinthians, Chapter 15 that gives a very clear picture about death.

This world is all we are accustomed to and most people have a fear of the unknown as they call it. Most will cling to life until the last minute that they have on earth.

When people appear in court they put their hand on the bible and swear by it.

This has been our guideline as a Christian nation. The bible goes back over 2000 years and is all we have to go on, but that poses no problem for me.

If you believe in God as I do, then you know that there is a better place waiting for you than this place called earth. We believe in eternity. Life everlasting. We never really die, we just go to a better place with no sickness, no wars, no pain. Only those left behind grieve and they are the ones to feel sorry for.

Paul puts it so nicely when he says, "Death where is thy sting, death where is thy victory." It is us who are victorious.

That's why I am not afraid of death. It is like closing one door and entering another dimension. My grand kids would probably say, "That's cool." It doesn't get any better than "cool."

Just the other day, a friend of mine told me that her mother-in-law had died. She put it this way: Tom's mom is standing with Jesus, touring heaven. Last night at 9: 30 pm she caught a flight. We saw angels surrounding her bed before she went. She didn't take any "baggage" and there were no security checks.

Departure was "on time." During her "flight " there was no turbulence.

She arrived at her destination with no fear, no tears, no sickness and a new heavenly body.

Then it went on to tell the funeral home where her earthly wishes were being handled.

I don't think I have ever read an obituary as beautiful as this. I hope this makes dying a little less fearful than it needs to be.

Weep for the living, not the dead. It is hard when a loved one dies because we miss them so very much, but what a comfort to know they are in a better place.

I find it very hard to visit a cemetery where my loved ones are buried because I know they are not there, just the earthly remains. My loved ones reside with Jesus and I know they are happy.

I will always have fond memories of the good times but I never want to dwell on the sad times. Life does go on and we have to pick up the pieces and make the best of it.

For all of you who loved your spouse like I did, don't feel guilty about finding someone to love. I admit I did at first but then I knew she wouldn't want me to be unhappy. You have to grab the brass ring and ride with it.

Someday we will be with our loved ones and there will be no jealously in heaven because it can't reside there.

I don't have all the answers and neither do the clergy but I do know He gives me peace day in and day out, sustaining me. That's all I need and that's all you need too.

You can spend the remaining days hugging clothes that belonged to your loved ones and starting each day with tears or you can keep the good memories and try to find happiness in your life. Every one needs someone to hug and share with. No man is an island. God wants you to be happy, don't disappoint Him.

CHAPTER 12

JOY IN YOUR HEART

Not to repeat myself but I can't say enough about the joy that fills my heart when I do something good for someone. I would like to share a few stories with you concerning this subject.

A few years ago around January there were two tragic fires to houses in my community. People were left without clothing, bedding and furniture.

Our church decided to act immediately to help these unfortunate people and opened one room near the class- rooms where they taught kindergarten. No one knew at the time what a headache this would be.

I was retired and after church services that day, I volunteered to work helping to sort the clothing that started to pour in. Well, we had a few volunteers the first day and then some volunteered to work an hour or two the days following but we were open from 8am until 4pm.

There were very few volunteers. Now many people from the church donated clothes and some furniture and some volunteered to pick up the furniture but only a few donated much time.

I was there from 8 to 4 every day because I was retired and had more time. It was hard work sorting all the different sizes and the little room was much too small but we made the best of it. Some of the women volunteers felt better that there was a male presence there because we started giving clothes not only to burn victims but anyone who was in need because we were getting an abundance of shoes and clothing along with bedding. Most people that came were very poor and I felt so good that we could help them. Many carried bag after bag because it was free.

One woman came there with a spring coat on and one of the volunteers knew her and told me later that this woman had lost faith in God for some reason (possibly because of a death in the family and she blamed God).

I had remembered putting a beautiful maroon coat away in the back of the room and something told me it would fit her. It was a warm coat for winter.

She didn't think I had her size but I told her I though it would fit and brought it to her. It was a real nice coat.

She tried the coat on and a smile came on her lips and her eyes got moist. The coat fit perfect but that's not the end of the story.

She reached into the pocket and someone had left a small wooden cross there. As she took the cross in her hand, she looked stunned. She gave me a smile, put the cross back in her pocket and thanked me so much. I had a feeling the thanks were for more than the coat. The cross had a new home.

It was a spirit filled week giving away clothes to the needy and I really felt like a salesman, except everything was free, which made it even better.

Two men who looked like they needed help had a ball picking out plaid shirts and some trousers that seemed to fit. They had four or five bags of clothing and asked if there was a phone where they could call a cab for their place was too far to walk with all those bags.

I pointed to my van nearby and told them to put their bags in it and I would give them a ride home.

They wanted to give me money for gas and tried to pay me a dollar. Of course I said no.

They thanked me several times. I felt like Santa Claus. I can't begin to tell you the joy that filled my heart that week.

You can give money and you can give clothing but it's not like giving yourself.

Even the bible in Galatians 6:9-10 says "Let us not be weary in doing good; for at the proper time, we will reap a harvest if we do not give up. Therefore, as we have the opportunity, let us do good…"

See, it was even popular to do good 2000 years ago. It's really not anything new.

Now I know most of you nice people out there don't need me to preach to you but sometimes we get caught up in our own world and forget the needy people around us.

This Thanksgiving we're going to buy a turkey and all the good stuff to go with a dinner and give it to a needy person I know.

She works hard but doesn't have much. You can do the same thing and it doesn't have to be at a special time of the year, people are hungry every day.

Nothing like "that feel good feeling " in your heart. You make God smile too. Remember, this is the day the Lord has made, let us rejoice and be glad of it. What better way than to give a little something back after all He has given us.

"Whatsoever you do to the least of My brethren, you do unto Me." Do you see Jesus in other people?

CHAPTER 13

POSITIVE THOUGHTS

These are some little sayings I've come across over the years and would like to share them with you:

If God had a refrigerator, your picture would be on it. If He had a wallet, your photo would be in it.

He sends you flowers every spring, and a sunrise every morning.

You can forget Him but He will never forget you. He waits patiently for you to come back to Him.

He has carved you in the palm of His hand.

He could live anywhere in the universe, and He chose your heart.

Face it, He's crazy about you.

Maybe some of you reading this book don't believe in Him, I've already said a prayer for you.

Always pray, God answers knee mail.

We used to have a saying in our prayer group: If you had been the only person in the world, He would have still went to the cross and died for you.

If I didn't feel His presence, I would be the loneliest person in the world.

Say nice things and learn to listen. God gave us two ears and only one mouth, so He must have meant for us to do twice as much listening as talking.

He who guards his lips guards his soul.

Stand up for something or you will fall for anything.

Do not worry about anything; instead pray about everything.

Be humble, remember, "Wisdom doesn't always come with age, sometimes age comes alone."

Do random acts of kindness.

CHAPTER 14

SOME OF MY FAVORITE PEOPLE

At any age in life we have favorite people that we admire. The ones that take your fancy tell a lot about you. I think Mother Theresa was a special person because she chose a life of poverty to be near people she could help.

Lou Gehrig was a favorite of mine not only because he was a great ballplayer and a good family man but because he knew he had a fatal disease and yet called himself the luckiest man in the world. He valued what God had given him even though he knew his life would be shortened.

I love country and western music so I have to say I admired Johnny Cash for his songs about Indians and spiritual songs he sang. He must have been proud of his country to record so many patriotic songs.

For movie stars, I admire Mel Gibson for putting up 25 million dollars to tell a griping story about Jesus even if it offended some people.

I admire young and old alike who are dying of fatal diseases and yet never give up.

Of course there are many more on my list but these are a few.

I'd especially like to tell you about my best friend called, John. He believed that to be a Christian, you have to follow in His steps. When John retired he spent all his time working as a volunteer at the Christian Care place. It was a place where usually the poorer people went either to get out of the cold or if they were depressed, John would pray for them. If John thought you were hungry he would give you his last dollar. I remember seeing him on his knees in front of an abortion clinic praying in all kinds of weather. His persistence closed the clinic down finally. If there were a prayer meeting taking place or a bible study or a rally for a Right to Life group, John would be there. He never could get enough of hearing about Jesus.

Toward the end of John's life he had a tumor on his brain and the doctors could only remove part of it. John, always a big man, became frail and needed a walker and someone to guide him.

I hadn't seen John in awhile until my wife passed away. In the funeral parlor that night, I saw him.

He was using a walker and a person was helping him walk toward me. I told him he shouldn't have come.

He told me that I should have known he would be there. Then he took my hand and said if I ever needed anything to call him. My eyes were blurred as I thanked him for coming.

One month later he was gone and I lost a dear friend.

He was never famous or held any important position. People never asked for his autograph or gave him a second thought but he was the closest man to Jesus I have ever known.

A year after he died I decided to write a tribute to John and put it in the local paper. With words to the best of my ability I praised him the best way I could. He was a man among men and I know God welcomed him with open arms.

If you have had good friends in the past but have lost touch with them by all means contact them and renew old friendships. Friends are too precious to lose and we only go this way once. Hold on to old friends and make lots of new ones. I can't begin to tell you how much I treasure my friends because they are a treasure.

I remember when I got through school and got a job at a local department store that I met two guys who became good friends. It was like the odd couple.

They both smoked and drank, came from rough families and chased girls. We were as opposite as ice cream and pickles. Maybe I was pickles, I don't know.

I do know that the three of us formed a bond together. The only thing we had in common is that we were all poor. I shouldn't say that because we had so much fun together.

They liked to go to bar rooms and I didn't, so they quit going. I was the one with the car and sometimes we would cruise all night just riding the streets and laughing a lot. We never did anything wrong.

After I met the girl of my dreams, we slowly begin to drift apart and I guess I lost track of them. I regret that to this day as they both died fairly young, but oh those memories. Nostalgia is sometimes very sad. Those guys were rough but they were my very best friends. Some people told me I was getting in with the wrong crowd but they were wrong. When I think back now, I really loved those guys.

One of them, back before I had a girl, really liked this one girl. They had went together before and got back together again. One day on my lunch hour she handed me a note

She asked me for a date. She was a pretty girl but I couldn't betray him.

He was a friend and I just didn't think it would be right to invade my friend's territory. I never told him about it because I thought it would hurt him. They started dating and seemed happy after that.

You have to treat friends with care like a piece of precious pottery. Handle with prayer.

On the subject of friends, do you have a friend you haven't heard from in years? Maybe you could look him up on a computer and relive old friendships. It might be worth the try.

CHAPTER 15

GREAT TRUTHS ABOUT GROWING OLD
(sayings someone else said)

1) Growing up is mandatory; growing old is optional.
2) Forget the health food. I need all the preservatives I can get.
3) When you fall down, you wonder what else you can do while you're down there.
4) You're getting old when you get the same sensation from a rocking chair that you once got from a roller coaster.
5) It's frustrating when you know all the answers but nobody bothers to ask you the questions.
6) Time may be a great healer, but it's a lousy beautician.

THE FOUR STAGES OF LIFE

1) You believe in Santa Claus
2) You don't believe in Santa Claus

3) You are Santa Claus
4) You look like Santa Claus

GREAT TRUTHS THAT ADULTS HAVE LEARNED

1) Raising teenagers is like nailing Jell-O to a tree
2) Wrinkles don't hurt
3) Families are like fudge…mostly sweet, with a few nuts.
4) Today's mighty oak is just yesterday's nut that held its ground.
5) Middle age is when you choose your cereal for the fiber not the toy

At age 4 success is….Not peeing in your pants.

At age 12 success is…..having friends.

At age 16 success is….having a drivers license.

At age 20 success is…..having sex

At age 35 success is…..having money

At age 60 success is ….having sex

At age 70 success is…..having a drivers license.

At age 75 success is…..having friends

At age 80 success is…..not peeing your pants

Remember always, that laughter is the best medicine, for when you don't laugh, you don't really live. Be a person that laughs at himself and can appreciate a good joke even on him. If you can't run with the big dogs, then stay on the porch.

I used to have a little saying that I pasted on the front of my bible. It said, "Jesus in me loves you." It reminds me that even if you're not a lovable person, Jesus loves you so I should too. Smile at your enemies, it will drive them crazy.

We shouldn't judge people until we really get to know them. It's like judging a book by its cover. Sometimes you might be right but most likely you will be pleasantly surprised.

I had to work one time for a new supervisor and I had dreaded this for a while. After a few months we had become very good friends. I was judging and I shouldn't have been. We need to give people a chance to show their real selves.

The Lord said, "Do good to those that persecute you." Well, nobody said it was easy to be a Christian but there are no alternatives.

Remember to say only the good things about people. A priest taught me that once and it is so true.

The bible says that our tongue is like a two edged sword so be careful not to cut anyone.

CHAPTER 16

DO YOU REMEMBER HOBOS?

If you're around my age, then you must remember the hobo who rode the trains illegally in boxcars. If fact there is a country and western singer called, "Boxcar Willie."

It was a nostalgic time when the old-fashioned coal driven " big monsters" went by my backyard and in the early hours of the morning, laying in bed I could hear the eerie sounds of the train whistle blowing announcing it's entry into the city. This is when the hobos would jump from the trains to avoid getting picked up by the police.

Many a morning when I went behind my garage, I would see hobos sleeping there. They never seemed to bother anyone.

I remember sending away for a newspaper called, "The Hobo News." It was a nice collection of poems like "Casey at the Bat" and

"The Wreck of Old 97." There were heart-warming stories of all kinds and it was only 10 cents. I really wished I had saved all those papers.

I think my love of poetry started after reading this paper.

I'd like to share some poems I wrote around this time when I was 11 or 12.

A HOBO TALKS TO GOD

A hobo knelt to pray one night
Beside a north-bound freight,
A solemn look was on his face
And his heart was free of hate.

" I'm making my last trip, you know
And I hope I'll be coming home;
I'm sick of the rain and snow
I no longer want to roam

" Oh, I'm not sorry you see
For any part of my life;
I've loved the open countryside…
I've known some misery and strife."

" But I've watched the sun come up each day,
And I've slept beneath the stars;
I've hiked along a country road
And seen this great land of ours."

"I've traveled far and near,
And with You always by my side,
I never knew the meaning of fear.
I served my country well,
Seen my comrades as they fell.
I never cursed my fellow man
Or wished for a better way,
I've always been close to You
And I've ate most every day.

I'm hoping You make a place for me
In the heavenly home above;
They say You judge a man real well
If his heart is filled with love.

Yes, I remember the hobos. It was a different era, a different time. They were fond memories and when I think about them, it gives me a warm feeling in my heart. The only way the younger generation will ever know the true story is for one of you seniors to tell them.

They might be more interested than you think. Tell them how the old engines sounded as they huffed and puffed and the sounds of the steel wheels trying to get traction as the coal was poured in the old boiler.

CHAPTER 17

MEMORIES OF DAYS GONE BY

How many of you out there haven't let you mind drift back to when you were a kid. Maybe you shared how things were back then with your kids or friends or maybe your grandkids.

I remember as a young boy lying on my back and staring up at the sky and the fluffy clouds that seemed to drift so peacefully through the sea of blue and I wrote this poem:

SHIPS IN THE SKY

Did you ever watch the clouds
        As they go drifting by,
Like a fleet of ghost ships
        On the sea up in the sky?
There are big ones and small ones
        And some as white as snow;

Tomorrow they may disappear
And you wonder where they go.
Like ships on a mission,
They sail far out of sight
And then like ghosts appear
On a dark and cloudy night.
They may choose to blot out the moon
And leave us in the dark,
And then disappear again at noon…
For a couple of days or more;
Sometimes they travel in groups,
Sometimes just one or two,
They seem to wander endlessly
Up in the sky of blue.

Oh, God must have had a reason
To put them way up there;
I guess He wanted to tell us
Our skies can't always be blue and fair.

When I was a boy as I told you, I had my first paper route when I was twelve. We rented a modest house, the bottom part. There were neighbors upstairs and you could hear them when they walked. We had four rooms and a bath with two coal stoves. My father drove a city bus for a dollar an hour and worked around 70 hours a week to make ends meet. When I graduated and got a job, I paid my parents room and board. We were poor, but my mom made homemade bread and baked beans I loved and we ate mostly stew meats and fish we managed to catch every Sunday and a few weeknights. I never felt underprivileged, maybe it's because my parents loved me so much, in fact, I felt spoiled because I was an only child.

My dad was 20 years older than my mom and he passed away years ago at the age of 85 watching his favorite Yankees play. My mom lived to be 93 and died just a few years ago.

A few weeks before she died, I had the startling revelation that when I was a boy I was poor. This is the poem I wrote and read at my mom's funeral mass. It pretty much tells about my childhood.

NEVER KNEW I WAS POOR

When I was a kid, didn't know I was poor,
There was this place they gave food out at the door;
They called it welfare, I guess.
My dad got a job working six days a week,
and my mom worked some too.
Didn't have TV or computers then, but there was always something to do;
Like horseshoes in the backyard and rollin' tires for fun,
And playin' baseball when summer vacation come.
Had high-top boots with a jackknife in them;

Nobody worried about hurtin' anyone.
Played hardball and played real mean,
Practice made me a hittin' machine…I was good.
Didn't have no uniforms, just a pair of cleats,
Old ones.
Played on an old field where we'd all meet.

My clothes didn't say, "Tommy Hilfiger or Old Navy,"
Just a faded old shirt my mom made for me…
And worn jeans, but they were clean.
Never thought I was poor.
My childhood was wild and free, got lots of hugs from my mom,
You see.
Teachers were strict and you got slapped some too,
But learned about integrity and the Golden Rule.

Had a big German Shepherd that we didn't own
But he stayed 10 years in our home;
Till' he died.

Bought my own bike at five dollars a week,
Peddled 100 papers around my street.

I know this might sound crazy, but we didn't
have time
To be lazy.
I was eleven at the time.

Had two wood stoves to heat our home,
Don't remember having any phone…
We talked to people face to face.
I had a great childhood and I could tell
you more,
I felt like a king with riches galore…
Never knew I was poor.

I got thinking about my big German shepherd awhile back and decided to write a poem about him. If you have ever owned a dog, than you can probably relate to this poem.

MY DOG

Sitting patiently with big brown eyes,
Always waiting just for me,
Wondering what adventure lies next.

Matters not if I'm rich or poor,
If he lies on soft quilts
Or just an old wood floor.

Always happy, laughing in his own way,
Loyal to the very end,

Taking life slowly, day by day
The best kind of friend.

Just looking for a pat on the head,
Rewarding me with a wag of his tail;
Giving love that never fails.

He grows quickly, this friend of mine,
Leaving his playful puppyhood behind,
Growing older along life's way.

Oh, those memories I'll always cherish,
Remembering his kiss on my face
And a friendship I can never replace.

Yes, he was here for such a short time,
Doggie years go so fast;
He gave his all, he was mine.

Don't think me odd if I shed a tear,
And relive old memories
Wishing he were here.

Years later, my son had a beautiful German shepherd that reminded me of my dog, Duke in the above poem. His name was Blazer. I used to love to go there for a visit and play with him.

When he died, I felt badly for the family and myself because I loved this dog

I went home and wrote a poem about him and it reminded me of the other dogs before him. This is the poem.

BLAZER

Blazer's gone to a better place, he's walking
by Jesus side,
He's gone to heaven to wait for us, it's like he
never died.
He's free of all earthly pain, he's gone to be
with God.

He was loyal to your whole family, a kind and
loving dog.
No dog had a bigger heart, it was overflowing
with love,
And the Lord knew he would suffer here, so He
called him up above.

Oh, we'll all see Blazer again, he'll be waiting
by heaven's gate;
We'll hug him and he'll lick our face,
And everything will be great.
For nine years he was a faithful friend,
But please don't feel so bad, because this
isn't the end.
He's playing up there with Duke,
Bullet, Sampson, Dino

And Brandy too,
For dogs, much like us, never die when their heart is ever true.

Sometimes nostalgia makes sad memories and copying these poems make me feel sad but they were good memories too. I said awhile back that I would never get another pet, but here I am now with three Siamese cats and a greyhound dog and am so glad we have them.

POEMS ABOUT WAR

Over the years of my life, there has been WWII, the Korean War, War in Vietnam, first and second war in Iraq. I guess wars have always been here throughout my lifetime. Now we fight a maybe never ending war on terrorism.

Like I said, when I was 11, WWII started, and I guess that's when I started writing war poems. This next poem is about WWII.

This is a different kind of poem. I could see a battle-scarred field after the war and I pictured a scraggly ugly thorn tree sitting there, the only thing left standing. I wondered if it could talk, what it would tell us.

THE THORN TREE

On a lonely, barren strip of land
Somewhere between Germany and France,
A single thorn tree grows....
Having survived the shells and tanks.
If only it could talk, the stories it could tell,
Of the men who fought and died
In their special kind of hell.

Yes, the thorn tree saw it all,
The brave ones and the cowards;
The young made old by war,
It watched them all fall.

It saw a soldier fall to the ground,
Looking for a hiding place;
Watched a mud-streaked hand
Wipe tears from his face.
The thorn tree saw it all.

It saw a private crying in fear
Afraid for his life.
It remembers a soldier scribbling a note

With hope it would reach his wife.
It saw a battled-hardened sergeant
Lying mortally wounded on the ground
Fighting death in his own silent way;

Not once uttering a sound.
The thorn tree saw it all.

It saw the dove of peace
Finally spread her wings,
And still the mighty guns;
It heard the freedom bell ring.
The thorn tree saw it all.

Yes, the thorn tree on this blood-soaked land
Watched soldiers fight, hand to hand;
Watched them fight and die,
Saw blackened gunpowder blot out the
sky.
The thorn tree saw it all.

Now the thorn tree stands alone,
Peaceful on this barren land;
The only thing growing for miles around,
As the restless wind blows the sand

The thorn tree waits in the warm sun,
With it's awful memories still in tact;
It hears the rumble of the big guns
And the tanks dreaded clickety-clack.
The thorn tree saw it all.
Settle down, little thorn tree
And rest yourself a spell,
You've earned some peaceful solitude
You've served your time in hell.

A couple of years later when the war was still raging and after seeing many war films, I wrote this poem about an American soldier whose life was spared by a German soldier who was his enemy. We were taught to hate the Germans for starting the war, but I thought, gee, can they all be bad ? They had to do what their country ordered them to do. My mom and dad taught me that there was some good in everyone.

THE CHOICE

On Christmas Eve in'44, I remember it like
yesterday,
I was on a reconnaissance patrol, when I lost my
way.
I stumbled through the night, fell and struck my
head,
And through a vision dimly, I dreamed that I
was dead.

When the vision cleared and I knew I was
alive,

I looked upward, in the barrel of a 45.
I heard a dreadful click, my body filled
with fright;
I knew death was inches away for me that
awful night.

His eyes then turned from me, and I followed his stare;
My wallet had fallen upright, the moon was shining there.
The picture of my wife and kids stared at him, as if to plea;
The grim lines left his face and he smiled down at me.

He helped me to my feet, wiped the dirt from my back,
Then he slowly walked away, and I knew he wouldn't be back.
I joined the medics after that, I couldn't fire a rifle again
For fear a bullet of mine might hit my enemy friend.

Now, every time there's a moon-lit night and the stars come out to play,
I wonder where that soldier is who helped me on my way.

I like to think that every soldier who gave his life and died on foreign soil will never be forgotten.

I know that God hasn't, nor their loved one's either. They paid the greatest price known to man. So I wrote a poem about one of them.

A FALLEN SOLDIER

A rifle and a helmet, stuck loosely in the sand,
Show where a young soldier made his final stand.
Just a rifle and a helmet in a strange and hostile land
Shows the tragic spot where he died like a man.
His body lies quiet and still as on the battle rages;
He has passed beyond the brink
And now belongs to the ages.
For God has lifted him up and held him in His arms,
And given him a haven against all worldly harm.
A rifle and a helmet marks an empty spot,
Where just a body lies, minus a soul and heart.

Here is a poem I wrote similar to the one about an unknown soldier and there were so many of them that didn't come back, not even their bodies. This was my tribute to them as a boy of 12.

AN UNMARKED GRAVE

In just one of a row of crosses,
He lies beneath the sod

He gave his life for Uncle Sam
        But his soul belongs to God.
There's no name upon the cross,
        His identity is unknown to man,
But he gave his life bravely
        For a freedom loving land.
He had fond thoughts
        Of someday coming home;
But now he lies on foreign soil
        Across the ocean's foam.

I guess you'd call him an average guy;
        Nothing special…maybe a little shy,
But he gave his life for a buddy you see,
        He became a statistic, another casualty.

He joined the tragic list
        Of those who had fallen before,
Just another number
        In a God forsaken war.
An unknown soldier
        Lying beneath the sod
Struck down in the prime of life,
        Known only to God.

As a young man I was in the National Guard and expected someday I might have to fight in a war and I wondered how I would feel about killing another human being.

Fortunately the Korean War came to an end and I didn't find out. Then about 20 years later our country fought in the far-east in Vietnam. This as you know was a terrible war unlike any other. We lost many men there and nothing seemed to be accomplished, but we should never forget those brave men who lost their lives there.

The only good thing that came out of this war was I adopted a beautiful little baby and now she is the mother of three great children, all girls.

In this poem, my thoughts might be like those who served in fighting.

A SOLDIERS CONFESSION

O God forgive me, I have sinned against my
fellow man;
I didn't want to kill at all but they sent me to
Vietnam.
They took me from my peaceful land

To a place across the sea and told me I
must fight and kill
If I wanted to remain free.
Just the other night, dear Lord, when the
shells were burstin' near,
I shot a Vietcong whose face was lined with
fear.
To my dying day, I guess, I'll hear his painful
moan...

I wonder if a loved one waits for him at
home?
Maybe a child or two is waiting to hear his
step;
I wonder…will I be in their debt ?
It might be different, you know, and I
could be lying there
With a bullet in my heart and dirt matted
in my hair.
They're not machines we're killing,
they're humans like
you and I.
And I pray for courage above, to my Lord up
in the sky.
Oh, I know I must kill the enemy for this is my
job;
But does this make it right…give me an
answer, God ?
Tell me that it's alright to kill, that I haven't
sinned at all,

But please don't let me see his face when to the
ground he falls.
Let's say a prayer for peace, so I can throw
away my gun;
Let me try to forget this war and the awful
things I've done.

There were a lot of "Dear John" letters during the war and no one knows how many hearts were broken of our soldiers who defended our country when their girlfriends grew tired of waiting for them. This next poem is about a letter to a soldier to inform him she had found someone else.

THE LETTER

A soldier crouched in a foxhole one night
To read a letter by the pale moon's light.
There was mud on the wrinkled envelope
But with it came much hope.
"Darling," was the way that it started,
"My thoughts have always been with you.
Since you've been so very far away,
But darling, I've found someone new
And I hate to break it this way;

I just couldn't wait another day…
I know you think I'm terribly wrong,
But you've been away so very long."

The letter slipped from his mud stained hand,
His fa ce was a horrible sight;
He cursed the war in Vietnam
And he cursed this dreadful night.
He closed his eyes and saw her face
And relived memories too hard to erase.

When dawn broke, his company charged
Right into the jaws of hell;
The bayonets glistened and the bullets flew…
Later, they found him laying there,
A blood stained letter clutched in his hand,
With these last words,
" Darling….I hope you'll understand."

During all the wars, soldiers wore identification tags that were known as "Dog Tags" by everyone. These were worn around their necks to identify a soldier. When a soldier was killed in action it was collected and sent home.

Uncle Sam always sent a letter explaining the death. I wrote this poem about a dog tag speaking.

A DOG TAG SPEAKS

I remember the day he first put me on,
Then donned the uniform of Uncle Sam.
They shipped us far across the sea
Away from his beloved land.

He was a man among men
Always wearing a smile;
He believed the Lord gave us a life,

And we should make it worthwhile

Oh, sometimes on the battlefield
In the stillness of the night,
I'd hear him pray to God above,
Praying to do what was right

He didn't believe in killing,
Not even the enemy you see;
He believed there was good in everyone,
He believed in eternity.

Then one night when the battle raged on,
And the shells were bursting all around,
I felt a fragment hit my chain;
And he fell wounded to the ground.
They separated us that night,

I left him all alone;
They put me in a letter
And sent me to his home.

Back at his loved one's home
The letter and I arrived;
Telling the tragic story
Of how her husband died.

But he's not dead, this I know
For up there in the distant sky
There's a place for men like him,
They'll never have to die.

A short while ago, I got to thinking about our flag and what she has meant to all the soldiers that were proud to put her on foreign soil. What comes to mind is the statue of the marines who raised the flag on Iwo Jima after much fierce fighting.

I remember the painting of Washington crossing the Delaware with the flag in the front of the boat, and one of the most memorable is when Francis Scott Key was trying to see if our flag was still there at the break of dawn. If your heart doesn't beat a little faster when you see it flying in the breeze then there is something wrong somewhere.

Johnny Cash when he was alive sang a beautiful touching song about a battered old flag.

This next poem is about an old veteran who remembers the flag and what she stood for. He is using a cane because of an old war wound and as he sees the flag flying proudly in the breeze, his mind drifts back and he thinks about his buddies who he fought with and how many never returned to their loved ones.

As I wrote about him, I could feel the love and pride he has for his country.

Have you ever watched a veteran how he holds his hand over his heart when our National Anthem is played. Every word of that song finds it's home in his heart. I silently saluted him.

WAVING...SILENTLY

In the courtyard
The flag flies each day,
Caressed sometimes by the gentle breeze;
People pass by and fail to see
The meaning and soul bared there.
The flag could tell stories never heard before,
The horrors of untold wars.

But today, no one cares,
Some want to burn her;
Others carry flags of their own,
Marching to a different drummer
While calling America their home.
The flag waits
For someone to look up…
And be noticed.

An old man
Aided by a cane,
Walks into the courtyard
Wounded and lame.
Sits on the bench to rest awhile,
Looks upward and begins to smile.

A lump fills his throat
And his eyes grow moist;
His heart fills with pride,
Remembering those who had died.

His buddies.

Died to keep the old flag wavin'…
Now it goes without sayin'.
Few think about the awful toll
That was paid in blood and tears;
Memories fade across the years.

The old man nods
As if to say,
Remembering another time,
Another year, another day.
Time passes,
The sun is dying;
The old man stands,
Sits his cane aside…
Closes his eyes,
Pays tribute to those who died.

His gnarled old hand
Rests across his heart,
His lips are mute,
He sheds a tear
In silent salute
To his proud old flag;
And then he is gone.

Men come to fold the cloth,
Part of the ritual.
She must come down before nightfall.
But there was a time…

Long ago,
She flew beyond the night
And only the glow
From the rockets red glare,
Let the world know…
Our flag was still there.

And no greed or hatred
No matter what,
Will ever be able to stop
Old Glory wavin' proudly on high.

Back when I was a teen, I was so proud of my country. I loved to read stories about how we won our freedom and became independent in 1776. I remember my dad going to see "Jesse James ."

This movie and two others were the only time he ever spent money at the theater. The other two movies were, "The Return of Frank James" and "Pride of the Yankees."

I wrote this following poem when I was about 16.

I'M AN AMERICAN

Are you proud to say,
I'm an American all the way?
Does your heart skip a beat or two
When "Old Glory's flying in the blue?

Are you proud of Betsy Ross
        And hard riding Paul Revere?
Are you ready and willing to fight
        For the things you hold dear?
Does the Star Spangled Banner give you a
        thrill?

Are you proud of the man who died on
        Bunker Hill?
Does it make you proud
        When you're passing through a crowd
To know that you were born free
        And live in the land of liberty?
Do you know our country's history
        And how we became free?
Does the Civil War make you fighting mad?
        Then you're an American, my friend
And I'd be proud to shake your hand.

CHAPTER 18

NOSTALGIA LAND

I'd like to take you on a trip to those good old days of the past that only seniors will remember and understand how very special those days were. Sure, then we didn't have all the luxuries that we have today but we had something more precious. We had integrity.

I guess this whole book is about the past. Even any young people reading this book sometimes probably think about when they were younger. My kids who are grown- ups now often talk about things that happened years ago so I'm not going to apologize. The good times should be remembered. It makes us laugh and maybe sometimes shed a tear, but that isn't all bad either.

I know I had a lot of good memories thinking about the old days. Even my foster girls sometimes talk about their past which wasn't always rosy.

I've already shared about the war years and when hobos rode the rails.

For all you people who love western movies and music like I do, I even wrote some poems about the old west.

I wrote poems about my kids and poems about my Lord. I'm not ashamed to tell you what a big role He has always played in my life. The only way you can find complete happiness is to open the door and let Him into your heart. As I said before, I'm not trying to preach a sermon, there are many people more qualified than me to do this but I couldn't write this book without Him in it. He said once, " I in you and you in Me."

Back when I was young and lived in Watertown, N.Y. way before urban renewal that left Public Square gutted and the areas surrounding it, there were many stores there. There was also a grand old hotel that had 100 rooms in it giving overnight lodging to many dignitaries. Across the road from the hotel was the birthplace for the J.J. Newberry store, a magnificent five and ten- cent store. It is still there but houses only a few offices in the building now.

I wrote a poem about this era and how it was at that time. I put it in the form of a ballad.

BALLAD OF WATERTOWN

I'm singing a ballad, a ballad of
Watertown,

I'm singing of days gone by, when
there were buildings all around.
When Public Square had character
with the Woodruff standing tall,
And six theaters adorned our town
to be seen by one and all.
The old Mohigan Store where old
friends shopped and met;
Where the butcher cut your choice
of meat and you could smell the
fresh baked bread.

I'm singing the ballad of
Watertown for everyone to hear,
Bringing back the memories that we
all hold dear.
When policemen walked the beat
and everyone knew their name;
They were of another era, it'll never
be the same.
Remember when the Air Brake was
still going strong, giving life to the

Oh it was a bustling place, old cars
everywhere, And J.J. Newberry's
stood proud on Public Square.

I'm singing the Ballad of
Watertown, before urban renewal
came along
To change my song of happiness to
one, big sad song. Remember when
the old trains ran down Factory
Street,
The only place in the nation to
establish such a feat. The trains
would come into the depot, their
passengers to depart,
To head to the Hotel Woodruff, a
building with much heart.

Public Square met all our needs,
something for one and all,
We got along just fine without the
Salmon Run Mall.
The fountain on the Square lit up
every night
With colors of the rainbow, what a
wonderful sight.
When doctors still made house
calls on their daily rounds.
Oh I'm singing the ballad, the
Ballad of Watertown.
It'll never have the character it did
way back then,
When the city was run by more
stalwart men.

It was a time before, "blue bags"
came along and Thompson Park
was free,
And children played outdoors
instead of watching TV.
Oh the Ballad was a pretty song of
good old days gone by,
Before the city fathers let Public
Square die.
They called it Urban Renewal.

Those were the days when there was activity on Public Square. Why I remember when I was nine or ten, my mom and dad would head for downtown as we called it back then, to park on a Saturday night when all the stores were open. It was better than TV watching all the different people go by and more likely than not, someone would come over to the car and start talking to us. It was a friendly town and still is but too much has changed.

I remember an old Irish cop talking to my dad one day saying he would give that car a ticket if he could spell, "Studabaker. I still laugh at that to this day.

When my daughter Kathy got married, she said she wanted me to say something on her wedding day. She had reserved a part for "A Father's Thoughts." I wanted everything to be just right, so I pondered over what I would say when I remembered a poem I had written about her, thinking back when she was a little girl and now would be getting married. Here it is.

WHEN YOU WERE ONLY THREE

Yesterday you played with toys
        And picked flowers on a hill;
Today you're wearing high-heel shoes,
        But you're my little girl still.

Your eyes are devilish as they can be,
        Just like they were when you were three.
Now you no longer play with toys,
        Your thoughts are filled with handsome boys.

Like the oak tree, you've grown quite tall
        And you'll need new clothes again this
Fall.
        Pretty soon a woman you'll be…
But I remember when you were only three.

        You'll marry a lucky fellow some day,
And if you're fortunate along the way,
        You'll have a little girl just like you
With strawberry hair and eyes of blue.

        But Father Time don't rush me so…
Please just let me be,
        With my golden thoughts of yesterday
When my little girl was only three.

Well, you've all had wonderful memories of your children, but I wanted to share this with you. If you're wondering about the poem above and what happened in my daughter's life, Kathy is happily married and the mother of five children. She has three girls who look like her and two boys. Her husband Al, is a good man and her kids lead a wholesome life.

When I was a boy of about 11 or 12 I loved to go sliding in the Winter time. I remember sand papering the steel runners on my sled so it would fairly fly. We didn't use saucers or tubes so much because with our sled we could steer it and knew where we were going. On brisk winter evenings when the ground was covered with snow, we would head for our favorite hill. The street- lights gave us all the light we needed. We would go there on weekends too. There must have been a dozen of us that would hurry through our supper and all meet to go sliding down this great steep hill. I just had to write a poem about it.

SLIDING DOWN THE HILL

Can you remember as a boy
When you slid down the hill?
What a lot of fun it was,
It always gave me a thrill;
Especially when we hit the ice

And took off like a jet
What a wonderful time we had
On the hill where we all met.
Our runners were so sharp
They glistened in the sun;
We fairly flew over the snow,
Nobody had more fun.
Our lungs were filled with winter air,
Our cheeks were rosy red,
No one will ever know the joy
We had with our trusty sled.
The memory of that gang of ours
Linger with me still,
When we all met together
To go sliding down the hill.

This next poem I wrote one day when I got to thinking about my childhood. I know we should live for this day but it doesn't hurt to think of the good times that happened when you were a child. In fact sometimes I think it is healthy to put your whole life in perspective and not just what we are now. Anyway, I wrote this poem quite a few years ago as I took my own little trip down memory lane.

MEMORIES

I visited my hometown just the other day,
To an old school house to watch the children play.
In my mind I turned back time
When I too, played there.
I thought of my friends I used to know
And wondered, "Where did they go?"
I remember the teacher who stood so straight,
How in her own little way she molded our fate.
Sometimes she seemed so demanding,
But there was patience too and understanding.
I feel I'm a better man today because she passed my way.

I remember a little pond just on the edge of town
With the rows of tulips all around;
And the little old lady who always had a smile,
Somehow, just knowing her made my life worthwhile.
I remember a little boy with a big dog
By his side,
How bad he felt when his dog died.

Well…I must shake the cobwebs free and

come back to reality.
For yesterday has passed away and new
memories fill it's place,
But every once in a while my memory drifts
to my childhood days
With thoughts too hard to erase.

I wrote what you might call a sequel to this poem. You see, I had a very happy childhood. I guess this proves that you don't have to have money to be happy. Yes, my parents were very poor but love conquered all that as it often does. I had a big German shepherd dog, friends throughout the neighborhood, baseball, horseshoes, movies and fishing that I truly loved.

My mom baked homemade bread, pies and beans. Now who could ask for more than that.

MEMORIES…AGAIN

I watched a boy playing ball and my memory
drifted back
To a flat sandlot field and a narrow cinder
track.
I thought of my childhood days and friends I
used to know,
The German Shepherd who followed me
everywhere that I'd go.

The years go by so very fast and boy
becomes a man
But he holds onto childhood dreams just as
long as he can;
For happiness is a little child with a grin upon
his face,
He owns the whole outdoors, the world is his
kind of place.
For him there are no wars or crime or civil
strife,
For there is only happiness in his small,
sheltered life
Oh to be a little boy again with wings upon
your feet
And joy within your heart, oh what a
wonderful treat
But boys grow to manhood and men rule the
world,
And childhood dreams are set aside, some
Other time to be unfurled.

The trip down memory lane is more real if you travel on a dirt road. When we were traveling into the nearest town the other day we saw an Amish buggy followed by about six cars. The horse was plodding along at its own speed. That really takes you back in time. Just seems like we're always in the fast lane and never take time to enjoy the countryside around us.

Too much TV and video games and kids aren't getting enough exercise.

I really have to tell you about the teacher I had in 6th grade. She was only about 5ft tall and kind of homely but boy did she ever have control of her class. I learned penmanship from her and she made me love poems and short stories. I actually loved going in her room because when she read to us she took us on a wonderful journey. Her voice was soothing and she made the characters jump right out at you. To this day I love reading books and writing poems and it is all because of her. I know there must be some dedicated teachers like her around.

For the sake of our young people, I certainly hope so.

CHAPTER 19

COUNTRY AND WESTERN LORE

Stop right here if you don't like to hear about stories of the old west. You can't walk down memory lane unless you talk about some of my favorite movie stars. For starters, lets go with John Wayne who always rode tall in the saddle. He was rough and tough but always fair and beneath that exterior was a soft heart of a saint. I know it was only the movies but every one I saw, I was the Duke and always got the pretty girl, or I rode off in the sunset which was pretty cool too. Whether he wore a big Stetson or the uniform of Uncle Sam in the movies, he was our hero.

What about Henry Fonda who just seemed to be born to be a cowboy with that soft Southern drawl. He could play a villain or the hero but you somehow always was on his side.

Jimmy Stewart was another great actor who could make you laugh or cry and he too made many westerns. Can you ever forget Allan Ladd in the classic movie, "Shane," Clint Eastwood in the "Ballad of Josie Whales" or "Pale Rider." Just to name a few of his westerns. I still like to imitate John Wayne when people ask me a certain question and I say, "Not Hardly." Who doesn't remember Clint Eastwood squinting his eyes that would bore a hole through the villains. Yes, the westerns took us back to when our country was still struggling to keep alive and the men who staked a claim in America. They fought Indians and bad men and the weather but they had the courage to move ahead to new boundaries to make our country what it is today.

We can never forget the men who died in the Alamo. Movies have brought the past clearer to us in the great westerns.

Just in the last few years, I started to write some western poems. The first one I dabbled with was a ballad. Now all of you who follow and listen to country music know that most songs are tear jerkers or something always seems to go wrong. The songs usually tell about cowboys down on their luck or they're about love that went bad or honky-tonk women.

But most people seem to like them and I guess you could call it beer drinking music. Juke boxes playing sad songs on a Saturday night. Well you get the drift anyway. Below is my first western poem, maybe you can put it to music.

A COWBOY BALLAD

I'd like to write a cowboy song about life gone
wrong,
About a guy and a jukebox and Saturday
night,
About cryin' in your beer feelin' sorry for
yourself
In a world that never goes right.
It's about loosin' your wife, your son
and your job,
And crossin' the law to the other side.
Spendin' time in prison with no place to hide;
Takin' your punishment and doin' the
time,
Strippen' years from your life for
Another one's crimes.

Oh I'm singing the cowboy blues
Life ain't pretty for me
But that's the way things are in
country.

Oh life ain't pretty but this I know,
As your eyes get hard and the muscles grow;

Lookin' twice your age and drowning in beer,
Takin' your knocks but showin' no fear,
Feedin' quarters in the jukebox on Saturday night,
Hopin' and praying someone starts a fight.
Blood shot eyes and a beard too long,
Listening to Elvis sing a love song.

Oh I'm singing the cowboy blues
Life ain't pretty for me
But that's the way things are in country.

Well, you're lonely and beat and the beer tastes stale,
Sorry for yourself, you keep drinkin' the ale.
"Drink up," you laugh and shout with glee,
Laugh and be merry , the drinks are on me.
But the song changes to another verse;
Just when you thought things couldn't get worse,
She walks in out of the night and your blood shot eyes take in the sight.
She floats across the floor with everything in place,
Soft round curves and an angels face.
"Buy me a drink" she says with soft red lips

And she slides on the stool with swivel hips.
She touches my arm and it feels like steel,
I must be dreamin', it can't be real.

"Play Johnny Cash singing A boy Named Sue,
Gimmie a quarter and I'll dance for you."
She glides on air across the floor and the look she gives me promises more.
I grab her waist and head out the door,
While the guys at the bar holler for more.

Now no more jukebox or Saturday night,
Stayin' home watchin' the kids is my plight.
But she's a honky tonk angel and can't change her ways,
The juke box beckons as night turns to day;
It's a cowboy ballad, what more can I say.

Oh, I'm singing a cowboy ballad,
Life ain't pretty for me,
But that's the way things are in country.

Well, I tried to get everything in that poem and when I read it to my kids they thought it was pretty funny. One of my daughters writes poetry and so does one of my sons so if they like what I write, it gives me some encouragement.

I think I would like to have lived in those days even without all the modern appliances we have today. You just improvise, that's all. Fireplaces and wood stoves gave off good warmth back in those days and lots of people today are going back to that type of heat. When you had a horse and buggy you didn't have to worry about the price of gas, you just had to feed it.

I remember going to visit my grandmother when I was about 10. We didn't own a car so my mom and I rode the train to within a mile or so of her house. We walked the rest of the way. My grandmother did not have electricity even though most everyone had it. It was quite an experience and I still remember when it got dark and she lit the kerosene lamps. She had a cook stove in the kitchen and I remember her taking the griddle off so we could toast bread with the old- fashioned wire racks. The bread was homemade and so was the butter, talk about a mouth watering breakfast, that was it. I can almost taste it right now.

We didn't have McDonalds then or Arbys or Wendys or any of the fast food places, but we did have home cooked meals that had real taste to them. We had homemade pies, fried cakes, and homemade cakes.

Back then we knew all our neighbors and they were all our friends. If you needed them for anything, they were just a yell away.

Summer evenings, everyone sat on their porch and talked to one another. It just seemed to be a different era, one that we'll never see again.

I have a leather wide brim hat that I bought one day in a store in the Adirondacks. Call it vanity, but I like to think I look a little like John Wayne in it. I've been thinking seriously of buying a pair of wide suspenders like the Duke wore too. Up here where I live near Croghan they fit in nicely with the local people. Every once in a while a buggy goes by with Amish people in it. It sort of transports me back to the old days. Why I even carry a red bandana in my pocket, because I don't really care for those little white handkerchiefs. Okay, call me a hick if you want but you can't really hurt my feelings, my skin is awful thick after all these years.

I used to love to read about Will Rogers and had an old beat-up book about him for years. He was a very witty man and everyone seemed to love him. In a way, I envied him. His jokes always had a good meaning behind them and he was never vicious. Just the other day a friend of mine sent me a quote by him. It goes like this: "Even if you're on the right track, you'll get run over if you just sit there."

When I was a young man I saw a western movie with Joel McCrae in it. Someone told me once he came from the Utica area. Anyway, he was a preacher in this story and the name of it was, “Stars in my Crown.” The title was taken from a song that went on to say that when each of us do something good it puts another star in our crown in heaven. I loved the song they sang and I really loved the movie. The preacher in it was a man of integrity. I want to share with you the poem I wrote from this movie.

STARS IN MY CROWN

When I was a boy there was a song going
around,
About a cowboy asking, “Will there be any
stars in my crown?
It seems you get stars for all the good things you do,
I hope someday that I’ll earn some too.
You know you’re supposed to help each
other along the way.

There’s a book on us that will be read on Judgment day.
It’s not a hard path He asks us to tread;
Just love one another, that’s what He said.
On the journey through life many people wait,
A loving word and a hug can drive away all hate.
A person is richer by far who has many friends;

Like the song says, "Friends are friends forever when the Lord's the Lord of them."

I see His face in the friends I have made,
They help me to face life, I am not afraid.

Yes I hope when the angel's trumpet sounds

That there will be many stars in my crown.

I loved it in the movies when the cowboys all sit around a campfire at night during a cattle drive and one of them would start playing a guitar and singing softly. I guess all my life has been filled with campfires from here to Vermont to Canada.

At church camp, Camp Aldersgate in the Adirondacks, we have a campfire every night deep in the woods with about 20 young campers and a guy named Bob plays the guitar and we all sing. It is a peaceful time at the end of day. We usually end by holding hands and saying a prayer. It makes you wonder how many people have gathered around a campfire to sing, tell jokes or stories about their life.

I thought I would write a poem of the campfire and tie it into life. There's something very peaceful about the warm flames and the scent of wood burning that starts you thinking. There is also a warm feeling as you look across the fire and see your good friends smiling at you.

I sometimes close my eyes and picture our Lord at the end of day sitting around a campfire and telling his disciples how beautiful the kingdom of heaven is and what they have to look forward to in that land of eternity. Telling them that He will be there too.

THE CAMPFIRE

Light one last campfire for me before I go,
Let me feel the warmth as it gives an amber glow.
Let me relive past memories as I look up at the sky
And gaze at the hot logs as the sparks begin to fly.
Reaching toward heaven.
I'll think of times gone by and try not to cry.

Oh there were happy times by the old campfire,
Old friends and family and stories we loved to tell.
There was a peacefulness there as the scent of pine cones filled the air.
Like perfume from heaven.

Just add another log so the fire won't die,
We'll sit quietly and some may even sigh…

With eyes closed.
Yes keep the fire going for another hour or so,
When it turns to ashes, then I'll be ready to go.

For life is like a campfire, giving warmth to
everyone;
It's good to feel a glow inside
When the day is finally done.
And we join our loved ones.

After writing my first western poem, I wanted to try another. I got thinking about one of my grandsons who when he was born seemed to have these very large ears. As time went by the rest of him caught up with his ears and he looked natural. For some reason or other, I started thinking about those real large ears and it gave me an idea for a poem. I would write about this tough little guy that had these big ears and people made fun of him until he couldn't take it anymore. It is a humorous poem, sort of like the song "A Boy Named Sue."

RABBIT EARS

He was born in a mountain shack, grew up
poor with just the clothes on his back.
And there's more…
Got all his growth by the age of eight,

Grew up with a chip on his shoulder, I mean a
heart full of hate.
To make things worse and to add to his years,
He had this scar on his face (a present
from his dad) and two big ears…
I mean big.
Didn't know the meaning of fear.
In his sock feet he was just five foot four
And there's more…
He'd walk into a barroom on a
Saturday night,
They'd look at his ears and his scar,
and yeah you're right…
There was always a fight, cause they
called him " Rabbit Ears."
He'd claw and tear and fight like a
bear, he knew no fear; More than once he
kicked ass, when they called him "Rabbit
Ears."

Whatever you do when you see him
sitting there,
In a lonely corner and nursin' a beer,
Just tip your hat and maybe say " Hi"
Take your beer and walk on by,
But don't ever stare at his ears.

I remember the night the juke box was
playin'
Country music, it goes without sayin'
But there's more…

The little guy was sittin' all by himself,
Away from the crowd like a little elf;
Then this mountain of a man walks through the door,
Lookin' for trouble, he was six feet four;
He went 200 lbs. or more…I mean he looked mean.
He walks to the table where the kid sat
With an empty glass starin' at his lap.
With a snarl he said, "I'm talkin' to you kid
I'm here for what you did…
To my brother that is."
"He's in bad shape I hear, just because he called you "Rabbit Ears."
"Which ain't no lie…they look like you're about to fly."

Everyone laughed…all but the kid
He raised his eyes from where he sit,
And there's more…

He stood up slowly, all five foot four,
His eyes were an awful sight,
Everyone knew there would be a fight,
A bad one too.
And only one would be standin'
When it was through.

Well, they took bets on who would win,
They all took the giant over him

But I took out ten
        And bet on the kid.
Well the kid hit him four times or more,
        Right on the nose,
And the big man's blood spilled out on the
        floor;
But there's more…

        The kid hit him twice, deep in the gut
Brought his short legs up
        And kicked him…well you know where,
And the giant started gaspin' for air.
        The kid jumped on the table and bit him
on the ear,
        Hit him again and the big man hit the
floor…
        And then there was no more.
Well, the fight only took a minute or two
        And when it was over, everyone knew…
You don't ever call the kid "Rabbit Ears."
        Whatever you do when you see him sittin'
there,
        In a lonely corner and nursin' a beer,
Just tip your hat and maybe say "Hi"
        Take your beer and walk on by,
But don't ever stare at his ears.

I had a lot of fun writing this poem and on talent night at the summer camp I read it to the campers and they seemed to get a kick out of it, that is, all but my grandson who happened to be there that night. After taking a little ribbing, he was smiling too. In fact he has grown to be a real handsome boy and no one would ever guessed that he had big ears at one time.

I once heard that in the old west when they formed a new town it was essential to have a drunk in it. Of course that might have just been folk- lore. What really inspired me to write the next poem was an incident that took place when I was working for the Gas and Electric Company. We were putting conduit under the walk on Court St. on a nice summer day. The street was blocked off from cars.

A man was staggering up the street with a brown bag in his hand that contained liquor and it looked like he had drank a good portion of it. As he approached us, he asked if we wanted some of his bottle. His voice was slurred and everyone laughed, including myself, I'm sorry to say.

At the time it seemed funny. As he was leaving, he stopped, looked around and said the words that I have remembered all these years. He said, "I've got a soul, too." Don't ask me what to make of it. I just know that his words touched my heart deeply. We sometimes tend to laugh at people because they are not like us. I'm not making excuses for people who get drunk, but maybe some think they have a reason.

This next poem I wrote was about a man who suffered a great loss and couldn't handle it so he drank to forget.

THE TOWN DRUNK

The old man lay in a drunken sleep,
An empty bottle was there by his feet.
As the people in town passed him that day,
They looked at him with disgust
And shook their heads in dismay.
Kids laughed and made fun of him
But he just looked up with a drunken grin.
He didn't care anymore.

Once he was married and had a family,
A beautiful wife and a boy of three;
But a terrible disease had come one day
And took his wife and little boy away…
And left him alone.
He found refuge in the whiskey and gin,
It helped him forget, it dulled his brain.

He sold his house and lived in a cheap room
Upstairs over the old saloon.
His beard was dirty and his clothes were too;
His washed out eyes were a faded blue.
He was handsome once.
Everyone in town seemed to know

The old man had sunk as far as you can go.

One day as he staggered down the street
He heard the loud sound of horse's feet.
He saw the little girl fall straight in their path
And with stamina he never knew he had,
He grabbed the girl and threw her aside;
That was the day the old drunk died.

And they didn't laugh anymore;
But there is one thing that the little girl swore,
She said she saw angels kneel there that day
And lift the old man up and take him away.

Now the body still lay there broken and torn
And people there failed to realize,
By giving his life he had been reborn
And now was in heaven with his boy and wife.
This is the story of eternal life.

We see people only on the outside but God looks deeper and sees the inside.

CHAPTER 20

WHAT DO YOU DO WHEN YOUR SPOUSE DIES

I am not a therapist nor have I ever had any training in dealing with a person's mind. I am not an expert in this field so you will have to draw your own conclusions. I can only tell you what worked for me. I know there are thousands of you out there who have lost a spouse and wondering how you are going to survive.

As I said earlier on in this book, I was married for 48 wonderful years to the most beautiful woman in the world. I dated her for over a year and we got married when we were both 21. We had six children of our own and adopted two. I was fortunate to have a good job and retired after 40 years. Almost six years after I retired, my wife was stricken with cancer and died three months later. To say I was devastated is putting it mildly. She was my everything, the love of my life. I mourned for over two years and cried a river every day.

I've already told you my story about going on the computer until I found a wonderful woman who was in the same boat I was in. Her husband also died of cancer five years before.

I'm not trying to say what worked for me will work for you but let me ask you some important questions. Be truthful with yourself.

1- Are you lonely for companionship, someone from the opposite sex?

If the answer is yes, then do something about it. Find out if there is a singles club in your area for older people like yourself.

Get a computer or use one of your friends. There are many real good sites out there and they will acquaint you with singles in your area. Anyone who has a computer can show you how. You make up a fictitious name and what kind of person you are seeking. No one has to know where you live until you get better acquainted and then you can share your email address.

Do you really want to go the rest of your life having no one to hug you or go places with?

Some will tell you stories about some awful people who get on the computer and in some cases maybe they are right, but I've found that the majority of people online are just like yourself, looking for someone to spend the rest of their days with.

2- If you're not interested in finding a mate that's okay. To each his own. Just don't sit around the house all day hugging your mates clothes or feeling bad. The harsh truth is they are gone and you are still here. You can be miserable every day or try to find happiness. Too much thinking is not good.

The most important thing is not to be alone too much. Go out for breakfast at your favorite diner or take in a movie. Shop till you drop. If you're a woman, get a new hairdo. Play cards, take a drive outside the city, walk in the park, get out of the house.

3- Remember, your spouse loved you and wouldn't want you unhappy. Feel the peace in knowing that they are in a beautiful place and are waiting for you, but you don't have to hurry to meet them.

4- Get rid of their clothes. I know this sounds harsh but it really isn't. Give the clothes to a needy organization. Let someone get some use out of them. Every morning I woke up I saw my wife's clothes and it started me crying again. You don't need this.

5- Always cherish the memories, the wonderful times you both had together, that's healthy.

This is the only life you are ever going to have. You can make the most of it or be unhappy the rest of your days. Some people like to go to a "Grieving Group" and be with others who have lost a loved one. If it works for you okay, but I didn't really need this.

6- Talk to the Man upstairs. He knows more than anyone else how you are feeling. Don't blame Him for your spouse's death. In this world we have diseases and tragedy. The Lord is the enemy of death, that's why He gave us eternal life. He'll give you the peace you are looking for.

He said, "Ask and you will receive." Take Him up on this. No matter how bad we feel, He never gives us more than we can handle.

It's a terrible thing to loose someone we love. Everyone who has had that experience knows what I mean. Life can hold much hapiness for us but unfortunately there is also sorrow. God did not spare His Son from sorrow so we know we will have some too. Sometimes it seems that some people have more than their share of unhappiness and I don't have the answer for you, only that if we can we should try to help ease the pain for them.

In the Bible Jesus makes a statement that I like to call, "The Eleventh Commandment." He says, "I command that you love one another as I have loved you."

Probably a feeling you might have if you do begin to go out with someone again is a one of guilt. This is a natural feeling but you should get rid of it. The wedding vows said, "Till death do us part." It doesn't mean that your new partner will be like your first wife. I have 8 kids and Linda never tried to take the place of my kid's mother. She is good to them and loves them very much and that's all that matters. It is a different era and things will never be completely the same.

I did find happiness again and you can too. We chose to become foster parents and that has paid big dividends. Valissa is happy and said we have changed her life big time. Le has come back for good and we now call her our daughter. If you want happiness you have to grab the brass ring and hang on for dear life. Enjoy the ride.

CHAPTER 21

I REMEMBER YESTERYEAR

Sometimes in the evening when the snowflakes are softly falling and I smell the aroma of wood burning in the stove, my thoughts drift back to another era I call, yesteryear. It wasn't a perfect time with the big global war about to begin, but it was a nostalgic time to live in.

It was an era of old cars and gas for nineteen cents a gallon at the sign of the Flying Red Horse. Girls wore bobby socks and men's shirts. They wore their hair in ponytails and wore saddle shoes on their feet (with the laces tied).

We had big bands with names like Tommy and Jimmy Dorsey and Woody Herman. Who could ever forget Harry James playing, "The Flight of the Bumblebee."

A skinny kid called Frank Sinatra and a pelvis swinging kid called Elvis had the bobby socker's swooning in the aisles. There were some "B " movies just like today but it was the era of great actors like Humphrey Bogart, Jane Wyman, Katherine Hepburn and Spencer Tracy to name a few. There were sex pots like Marilyn Monroe and Rita Hayworth too. We had comedians like Bob Hope and George Burns. There were crooners like Bing Crosby and Dean Martin and a sarong girl named Dorothy Lamour.

We had a champion swimmer who turned actress named Esther Williams, a genuine Tarzan named Johnny Weismuller and western legends like John Wayne , Gene Autry and Roy Rogers.

It was the time of the Andrew Sisters and the silky smooth sounds of Nat King Cole.

Movies didn't need ratings back then because they were fit for the whole family. Hollywood has really come a long way. We saw double features, plus news and cartoons. They were black and white movies but we didn't care.

It was the time when the quiet evenings would be shattered by air raid sirens bringing everyone back to the reality of the big war. It was the era of the railroad with their huge black monstrous engines puffing smoke furiously, the pig pistons churning and the wheels slipping on the shiny tracks fighting for traction and finally making headway as the coalman fed the hot boiler. It would pull their 100 or so freight cars across this great country of ours, and as always carrying their unwanted guests, the American hobo. I remember late at night hearing the eerie lonesome wail of the whistle blowing as it steamed along the way.

Yesteryear was the time when radio was still king with the black and white TV looming on the horizon. Radio was famous for programs like the Shadow, Tom Mix, and Jack Armstrong, the all American boy. It was the time of apple pie and Chevrolet. I remember my dad buying a 1929 Chevy for $10 to transport us fishing a few miles from town. I learned to drive on that old car with the long stick shift and a clutch on the floor. We kept the car three years and my dad sold it for $90, how's that for making a profit.

I remember my dad getting a set of real horseshoes, not the store bought kind. On warm summer evenings, the neighbors would gather in our backyard and we would have horseshoe tournaments. I practiced until I could throw with the best of them. Oh the fun we had and it didn't cost a cent.

When I was a boy, everyone played hardball, not that sissy game today with a softball. You had to hit a ball thrown around 80 miles an hour or you didn't play. There were no second-string players because everyone could hit and field real well. I remember a couple of guys I played against ending up in the major leagues.

Back then there were only 8 teams in each league, and no free agents or "wild card teams." The Yankees were a dynasty and the "Bums" from Flatbush and the Giants from the Polo Grounds were usually the rivals come World Series time. It was called the nickel series or subway series.

The games were played in the afternoon and a lot of kids played hooky to listen to it home on the radio.

No one ever heard of Aids. There were no rock stars then performing half nude with long hair to their waist. We had our heroes and nobody wanted to burn the flag. We had dedicated school teachers that taught common sense and everyone got the same diploma. You either passed or you didn't. They weren't a bit shy about having a kid repeat a grade if he didn't know the work. They never gave you a watered-down diploma.

We had big families, covered dish suppers, block dances and a strong belief in God. At Christmas time the manger scene was displayed on public property for everyone to see.

I remember taking my best girl to the movies and they always had a vaudeville act before the picture started. The old theaters had brass railings, high back seats and later on, three- dimensional glasses they would hand out. It only cost a few bucks to take her out and you hardly ever kissed her on the first date. We had a beautiful park where you could see the whole city and that's where the cars parked to kiss and hold hands in the late evening. You courted a girl for a year or so before proposing and on the wedding day she was dressed in white and more so than not, a virgin. Family life meant something and marriages lasted back then. Somewhere throughout the years, we lost something very precious. Could it be because we don't want God in our schools or court houses .

The clothes-lines in America's back yards were filled with clean sheets and work clothes dried by nature's breezes with the fresh smell of the outdoors. I remember on real cold days, my mom bringing in my dads work pants frozen so they would stand by themselves. We had ice boxes filled by the men who drove stack rack trucks, their shirts dripping wet from the blocks of ice carried on their shoulders with the ice tongs.

The American people were a hearty lot back then, proud of their country, their heritage.

I remember a quiet Sunday morning, December 7, 1941 when the Japanese pulled a sneak attack on Pearl Harbor. This ignited World War 2. American's, with sleeves rolled and fighting mad were a determined lot. They worked around the clock in defense plants all over our nation. Men and women worked side by side for one common purpose, to crush the

Axis war machine. The name, Rosy the Riveter was given to the females who did men's jobs making planes and tanks for our fighting force. There were only older men and those who couldn't pass the physicals left to work in the plants too. The year 1941 saw a corn cob smoking shrewd old General called McArthur vow to return to the Philippines which he did after 5 years. The war saw General Eisenhower affectionately known as "Ike" take command of our armed forces and later become president of our country. The cry, "Remember Pearl Harbor" echoed throughout the land much like the same cry of the Texans almost one hundred years before which was "Remember the Alamo." Young men volunteered to fight and die for our country. We learned to hate Adolf Hitler and his goose-stepping war machine, along with Mussolini and Hirohito.

We stuck together for the cause of freedom and finally "D" Day came and we invaded Europe for the final push, liberating thousands of Europeans. Shortly later, the "Atomic Era" was upon us and President Truman made an important decision to save American lives. He had to drop this terrible bomb and destroy many Japanese. The effect would not wear off for another 20 years with people still being affected by the radiation.

The war ended and people all over the world danced in the streets, crying and hugging each other. I had just finished playing ball at Knickerbocker Field when we heard sirens wailing loudly all over the city.

I became part of that huge crowd on Public Square wedged so tight together nobody could move. We hugged and kissed and I can't remember a time in my life when I saw so many people so happy. We were one family then and we were all Americans and proud as we could be. This was America in its finest hour.

Defense plants converted over to auto factories again and the Ford Company made a high priced lemon, the Edsel. Cars had design and chrome and class, not like the matchbox effect of today's look alike tasteless models.

I remember a car backing into my 1937 Buick hitting the front fender. I took a hammer and pounded it out because it was real metal, not like today's cars with their fiberglass front ends. They rip like paper.

Yes, I remember when railroads were going strong, cars had class, teachers were dedicated, and families had roots that ran deep. We believed in the motto, "In God We Trust." Everything wasn't always rosy but we stuck together knowing we could lick anyone or anything that threatened our freedom.

I remember yesteryear fondly. It doesn't mean I don't enjoy life today but everything has changed so much, most of it not for the better. I'll never forget my teacher saying, "We got to get back to the basics." This was yesterday teaching us the basics.

CHAPTER 22

TRAVEL

If you're still in pretty good health and have been taking your pills everyday (mine are up to 8 per day) then this is a great time to visit those places you've always wanted to, before you pass into that Great Beyond. Keep in mind always that you only go this way once and you deserve the very best.

If you've still got a little nest egg left, then use it on you. Spend your kid's inheritance. Go on a cruise to Bermuda or the Caribbean. Remember those series of "The Love Boat?" Sounds like fun, do it then. Fly to Florida during the winter months. There are many options out there.

If you love nature, what more beautiful place to go to than Alaska. In the nice weather of course.

OK, you haven't saved up that much and your pension is sparse, I've still got good news for you if you drive a car and most of you do. I've run across some of you in my neck of the woods doing 37 miles an hour. Just kidding. Actually, when I drive, we move right along at about 5 miles over the speed limit. This way the troopers don't bother you.

Northern N.Y. has many beautiful country roads just a few miles from me. In an hour and a half I can be in Lake Placid, the heart of the Adirondacks where the beauty is breathtaking. If I travel the other way I can enjoy the St. Lawrence River and take a nice cruise very cheap. I can visit nearby Vermont or Canada all in a day's journey.

I'm not trying to be a travel bureau, just showing you how to enjoy God's wonderful creation when you have all the time in the world and don't have to worry about being to work the next day.

Wherever you live there's got to be great country not too far from you. Explore it.

It is always better traveling anywhere with a companion. At least that is my opinion.

If you don't like to drive, take the train or a bus ride. Many older groups get together and plan a nice tour. If you can't find a companion, this is a great time to take a grandkid with you, one on one. Give them the time of their life, they will remember it forever. On this subject, try to get closer than ever to them, they need to have a grandmother or grandfather in their life, don't get stagnate. You can't use the excuse anymore that you are busy, because if you don't have time for them now, you never will. Did I make you feel guilty? I tried too.

If you don't have any grandkids near you, then ask to take a kid that belongs to a friend of yours. Most likely the kid will be happy to go with you on a new adventure. I love kids and I have a good time when I'm around them. From a little infant to teen-agers, they can be a real joy.

You can be a person they talk to when they are troubled. Sometimes they like to talk to someone outside of their parents and you can listen and be there to give them the right advice because you've probably been in the same situation before.

One time there was an older gentleman in our prayer group who shared something with me. It seems a young girl needed someone to talk to so she picked him. He said for an hour she talked about her problems. At the end of that time she thanked him so much for helping her but he had never said a word. You see, he was just there for her.

Now if you've never flown anywhere and always wondered what it would be like, this is a great time to do it. Take a young friend, old friend or companion with you. If you still have your spouse, give them a second honeymoon somewhere secluded. Don’t say you’re too old, just because there’s snow on the roof doesn’t mean there isn’t a fire going inside. Live like today is the last day.

CHAPTER 23

FOR MEN ONLY

I knew you women would look at this chapter, and as for you men, get your mind out of the gutter. It's not that kind of a chapter. Actually I said for just men because I know all you women know how to cook. God forbid, if you haven't learned by now. Some of you men have some knowledge of cooking but now is the time to really dabble into some recipes you have never tried.

Watch some TV shows on cooking different things and then invite friends over for dinner to share with you. Great conversations happen over good food. For you men who are all alone, now is a good time to ask that attractive widow over for dinner. Tell her you would like her opinion on a new recipe you just tried out. If this works, next time will be easier and then you can light candles, don't push it.

If she has a lady friend, invite them both over the first time or make sure one of your relatives is there for the first meal. Put a little cologne on but don't take a bath in it. Hold the chair for her at the table. Women just love men with manners. If your meal is real good, next time try something different.

This chapter probably could be titled, "Recipe for Living" because happiness is eating a great meal. Learn how to prepare something unusual and invite people over to enjoy it. What better combination than good food with good friends. Your neighbors will start calling you, "Chef."

I'm not trying to make this into a recipe book because there are hundreds out there but I really have this nice tomato sauce I make that I would like to share with you. It's my own recipe and you won't find it in books.

I use a crock pot.
3 or 4 large cans of crushed tomatoes (depending on size of crock pot)
1 jar of Alfredo creamy sauce
1 can of tomato paste
2 tablespoons of sugar
½ cup of grated cheese
Put above ingredients in crock pot and turn on low.
In a frying pan cook 3 lbs. chop meat until brown

2 large onions diced
1 clove garlic minced
Put garlic and onions in frying pan with chop meat until cooked
Drain grease
Put chop meat, onions and garlic in crock pot
Add grated cheese
Mix good and let cook on low for around 2 to 4 hours. You can sprinkle a little parmesan cheese in it and stir.

Cook spaghetti or ziti or macaroni and put sauce on top.

Sauce can be used for making lasagna too. Whatever sauce is left over, freeze until another day. It's delicious at any time especially with Italian bread. The aroma that fills the house is wonderful. You could turn the fan on in the summer and make the neighbors drool.

The idea is to put something original together so people will think you are a genius. Explore. That's the secret of being a good cook, anyone can boil water. The way to win a woman over is through her stomach. They always said that about men, but women are no different.

The summer is a great time to have friends over to BBQ. Put a chefs apron on and act like you know what you're doing. Grilled meat is very delicious whether it is steak, chicken, hamburgers or hot dogs.

Get a rotisserie. It makes wonderful tasty chicken, pork or prime ribs. All the fat drains off into a tray which makes it healthy too. It has a basket for smaller pieces of meat and one for potatoes and vegetables. Guaranteed excellent meal every time.

CHAPTER 24

LONELINESS

I think one of the worst diseases in the world is loneliness. You have lost your spouse of many years and now you feel so helpless. For almost three years after my wife died I felt this way. I was married for 48 years, but it doesn't matter how long, you are suddenly left alone with nothing but memories and you still have some years ahead of you. Every morning you see their clothes in your bedroom or closet and the pain starts all over again. I had 8 kids to help but the times I was alone were the worst. Every morning I woke up in the same bed we shared and the hurt started all over again. Tears would roll down my face and I couldn't stop them. I was actually afraid the stress would start my ulcers up again. When my wife was dying I was so stressed out, it brought on bleeding ulcers and

I needed 5 pints of blood before coming home from the hospital. After all those years of closeness and happiness I didn't know where to turn or what to do.

Does that sound familiar to some of you out there? I already told you the story of Linda who I am married to now and how I changed my life around and found happiness again.

After Linda lost her husband to cancer she felt the same way I did so we had a lot in common. Maybe some of you widows out there can find a nice man who has lost his wife and do some things together.

Linda formed a group of women and they called themselves "The Winthrop Women." I laughed when she told me, and all I could think of was, "The Stepford Wives" after the movie of course.

Linda and the women who were without spouses would meet different times and play cards, go to dinner or the movies. The idea was to have companionship and not be alone. This worked pretty well for all of them, especially those who really didn't want male companions.

Too much being alone isn't good unless that's the way you want it. Everyone marches to a different drummer. I think I speak for the majority when I say that the real loneliness won't go away until you find a mate. You may be getting along fine, or so you tell people, but if you were married before, there is that craving to be held again and feel close to someone of the opposite sex.

Most of the widows have told me that they are lonely but don't know what to do about it. They feel shy and guilty about meeting someone and don't feel it is worth all the bother. A woman from Rome that has been corresponding with me for over two years is a widow who lost her husband quite a while ago. I knew her even before I met Linda. She has had a few dates and not until recently did she find someone she cares about. The outcome of that is still to be seen. She felt guilty and many times didn't think it was worth the bother but this time she seems to have found love. You know the old saying, "Better to have loved and lost than never to have loved at all."

The love sites on the computer are full of stories about lonely people who finally found a match. No two people are alike and if you are a widow you aren't going to find the replica of your husband, but you just might find a man who will put the spark back in your life and treat you like a queen.

Look, life itself is a gamble. You don't have to marry the first person you date. If you go out enough you will feel chemistry with someone sooner or later. There are a lot of very fine seniors out there that just want someone to spend the rest of the time they have here on earth with.

I traveled 70 miles one night to a singles dance club. This was scary because I have two left feet when it comes to dancing. No one ever showed me how to dance. They gave you a few tickets of the opposite color and women would give you a ticket of a different color to exchange. Then you danced with them. I will say that a lot of women left that night limping.

The good news was that I got to hold a lot of women real close and talk to them. What really made me envious was there was this real slim old guy about 80 and he could dance. He was swinging some pretty women around and never missed a beat. I silently cursed my teen years for never learning.

I have to tell you about this singles club for seniors that was forming in our area. I read about them in the paper and gave them a call. The next night they were having a picnic at the park and I was invited to come. Even at my age I was a little shy. I had been out of circulation for almost 50 years. I drove up to the park with my 10 year-old granddaughter, Desiree and looked down where they were holding the picnic.

I suddenly got the idea to send my little girl down to scout for me and to report back if there were any possibilities. It was so funny seeing her walk past all the women and checking them out. After about 5 minutes she came back and gave me the thumbs down.

I had about 4 dates that were all flops. No chemistry for me or for them either. The women who did appeal to me lived just too far away. I was real discouraged until I met Linda online and three months later we were married. Don't give up, it can happen.

I just can't believe you are happy with your loneliness. Please try to find a companion to do things with and have fun.

When I was on one love site for singles, I decided to browse all the women over 60 who were trying to find a mate. On this site there were around 900 or so wonderful women who just wanted to spend the rest of their life with someone who would hug them and make them feel alive again. They wanted a mate to travel with, take them to restaurants and church and spend quiet evenings with.

The important thing to remember is that you are alive. It is very sad that you lost your spouse but you can't do anything about that now. You deserve lots of happiness and most of all, love. Don't cheat yourself of the days you have left.

CHAPTER 25

HE LEADETH ME

Maybe some of you won't want to read this chapter thinking it is too religious. I have to write this because I can't stop talking about Him and how He has guided my life.

From my earliest recollections of my childhood to where I am now He has led me. It has been a life of happy memories, a happy childhood, a happy marriage and after losing my loved one He has given me new life and another chance at happiness.

If He were to call me tonight I would have no regrets knowing He has prepared a place for me with Him. I love every one of my 8 kids and 15 grand kids and feel I have been very lucky to such a joy filled life.

He has placed in my heart a love for people, for the mountains and woods and has given me a talent for reaching young teens.

Probably the only talent I have but I thank Him for this.

My happiest days have been teaching confirmation classes, doing devotions in the outdoor church in the woods and helping promote youth rallies in our prayer group. Just recently as I have shared with you, He has placed teen girls in my house to give them love, home life and a sense of belonging. It has paid off big time with wonderful results because love can break down all barriers. He filled my heart with love so I could give it away.

He has filled my heart with music again and I try to live everyday for Him. That is my purpose in life. Everyone needs a purpose to exist.

My first wife used to love the verse that says, “Because He lives, I can face tomorrow.” It is so important that we know where we are headed after we leave here. All our good deeds precede us.

Send a lot ahead of you.

I wrote a simple poem one time about the birth of Jesus that I would like to share with you. You see, I put my feelings better in the form of a poem. I got thinking one day how this little baby was born to a young girl on a cold winter night in a lowly manger and it makes me feel very humble that He would have His Son born like this. I tried to put it into words.

THE WORD MADE FLESH

God's voice rang out in song one night;
A new star in the sky beamed out it's light.
A gentle girl said, "Yes" and a new era was born;
Wise men followed the star in the early morn.
Pagan Kings trembled, shepherds quaked,
A Savior is born for our sake.
A small cry pierces the night
Angels sing with all their might;
Darkness yields to the light.

God smiles, it is done….
He gives to mankind His only Son.
Love flows down from Heaven,
Sins are about to be forgiven.

A Savior born to pay our debt,
To die upon a tree
In a place called, "Calvary."
A wasted life?…and yet…
Necessary for you and me.

The Son died to please His Dad;
The ending seems so very sad,
But, lo, this isn't the end of the story…
God raises His Son to eternal glory.

As I have said before there was a short time after my wife died that I was angry with Him for taking her away. I prayed for Him to take me and leave her here because a mother is something very special. Not to take anything away from fathers, but kids really need their mom. I wanted to change places with her. You see I had missed the real important point of our time here on earth. It really doesn't matter how long we live when there is a more beautiful place waiting for us.

Are the real fortunate ones the people who live to be 90 and have their bodies wracked by aches and pains or the ones who die at 70 or earlier and have always been in excellent health? I used to visit shut-ins and give them communion on Sunday morning. Some of the ladies were in their late 80's or over 90. All of them wanted to go to heaven and be with their loved ones. The fun had gone out of their life and it was time to move on to a better place.

There was this one old lady named Phoebe and her husband had died 30 years prior to her. Her whole conversation was always about him. I said to her one morning,

"Phoebe, do you know what your husband is going to say when you finally join him?" She shook her head. I said, "He's going to ask what the hell took you so long?" She laughed real hard.

The point I am trying to make is that sometimes you can be here too long. Is it a wonderful thing to live to be 100 if the quality of life is gone? Let me give you an idea by sharing this poem I wrote.

LIFE

He stared out the rain- streaked window
Of his one room nursing home;
His eyes were moist like the window pane
And he felt so all alone.
He turned 80 the other day and his hands
were wrinkled and old,
He closed his eyes and thought of better days
as he watched his life unfold.
He saw himself as a young boy playing with all
his friends,
Without a care, never realizing that this is the
way it would end.
He saw a handsome young man courting a
maiden so fair,
Remembering her ruby lips and the gold in
her soft hair.
He saw his young kids and how they hugged
him so tight.
He remembered feeding them when they
woke up at night
And he could still feel their bodies as he held
them close in his arms,

Vowing silently to protect them forever and
keep them from all harm.
He saw a big old house where laughter filled
the air,
Kids coming home from school, their episodes
to share.
Then one by one they left his happy home
To start a life anew, and raise a family
of their own,
Leaving just the two of them feeling so
alone.
Then the angels came and his wife left
him too,
Taking away his everything but there was
nothing he could do.
The rain stopped and with his knarled old
hand…
He wiped away a tear and tried to
understand.

I don't want to sound too morbid but I remembered my mom in her last years in a nursing home because she needed 24 hour care. She died at 93 but for the last five years she was just existing, so how do you measure your time here. She called her room, San Quentin.

Store your treasures in heaven where they cannot rust. Let your light shine so that others may see your good works.

I have a Japanese lady friend who started corresponding with me after I got married. We invited her to lunch one afternoon and she rode for hours from Brooklyn to meet us and spend a few hours sharing with us. She has 5 children, is divorced and saw my profile on a love site that I thought had been deleted. Linda and I love this woman like a sister. Her mother still lives in Japan. She works in the soup kitchen in Brooklyn doing volunteer work and shares with us how rewarding it is. She helps young Japanese students who can't speak English.

Do you wonder why I say I love my computer. It takes me to Norway to visit a young mother to be whom I love like a daughter and transports me to Ohio to share with a friend I have known since she was a teenager. It takes me to the home of a six year old boy whose body is in a cast and whose 16 year old sister is one of the sweetest girls I know. On my computer we talk about God, family and good and bad happenings in our life. It brings me closer to new friends I have met like a woman named Terry and her twin sister Janet, what lovely people. It makes me feel like we are all one in Christ.

Yes, He has been leading me all my life and doing such a tremendous job.

Just the other day my wife and I were at a craft show and there was this young lady selling candles who looked familiar to me. I asked her if I knew her. A smile came on her face and she said my name and we hugged each other. Her grandmother used to bring her to the prayer meetings years ago when she was a young girl. We had a great talk and she gave me her email address so now I have another friend to add to my address book.

Look, I know some of you older people don't want to get a computer but before you say no, let someone who owns one show you how it works.

When I got mine I couldn't even type and to this day use only one finger but I cannot tell you enough about the joy it has brought me. I even talk to my friends on instant messenger. It sure beats writing letters.

God has given me such wonderful friends it would be an injustice not to keep in touch with them. Computers make it so easy.

Every morning when I wake up we have our little talk and He puts my mind at ease. I can go to Him with everything. He told us in His book, "Ask and you shall receive, knock and it shall be opened unto you." He opened the door to happiness and outside that door is what life is all about. The Lord will take the loneliness away if you just ask. He did for me.

I think one of my favorite songs is, "He Touched Me." The other part of it says that I am no longer the same. He changed me.

We are all in the same boat and sometimes the seas can get pretty rough and we have to hang on to one another for comfort. The good news is we have a Captain at the helm that knows where the shoals are. Did you know he can even calm the sea? Like the old song says, "Put you hand in the hand of the Man who calms the water" and He will lead us to a safe harbor.

People are dying to get out of this world. Don't be afraid when the time comes, to "Let go, let God."

CHAPTER 26

LEAVE SOMETHING FOR YOUR FAMILY

When I say leave something, I'm not really talking about money. I'm talking about something they will cherish much more and it really doesn't cost very much. Let me share with you what I did and what you can do. You might not even have thought about it.

Write a letter to your kids or grand kids telling them some of your thoughts and what you believe in. I made a cassette and recited some of my poems and one of my granddaughters was playing it the other day.

This book I am writing is for my family too. I hope it will be published because I want to share it with everyone, but if it isn't then at least my family will have copies.

If you're good at photography then leave pictures that you treasured to your loved ones.

If you paint then do the same. Share your works with the family.

You men or women that are carpenters, make a bird feeder or a birdhouse or anything to hand down to your family.

Of course the best thing to hand down is the time you spent with them. Take a lot of pictures with you in them.

If you're a good cook, put together all your recipes and give them to the family. I still would like to know how my wife made that delicious homemade bread.

If you have a green thumb, tell them your secrets. Now I know your family will remember all the good times you have had together but it always is nice for you to give them a little something extra.

A good friend of mine is writing what she calls a journal. Things she wants to put on paper for people to see. You might even have a good time doing this.

How about all you women who have the great talent of knitting, making blankets or scarves or mittens for the grandkids? Probably most of you have already thought about these things but just thought I would refresh your memory.

Leave some of your works with them. You don't have to hurry to leave this earth, just have everything ready when you go.

I remember my father trying to play the new harmonica he had bought when I was a young boy. One of my daughters is very musical so awhile back I gave this to her and she has learned to play some pieces on it.

Your children love you and treasure anything you can leave them. Leave a legacy of love for your family.

CHAPTER 27

WHAT IS A GRANDPARENT?

A friend of mine sent this to me on my computer. It is taken from papers written by a class of 8-year olds. This might give you an idea of how your grand kids look at you.

Grandparents are a lady and a man who have no little children of her own. They like other peoples.

A grandfather is a man grandmother.

Grandparents don't have to do anything except be there when we come to see them. They are so old they shouldn't play hard or run. It is good if they drive us to the store and have lots of quarters for us.

When they take us for walks, they slow down past things like pretty leaves and caterpillars.

They show us and talk to us about the color of flowers and also why we shouldn't step on cracks.

They don't say, "Hurry up."

Usually grandmothers are fat, but not too fat to tie your shoes.

They wear glasses and funny underwear.

They can take their teeth and gums out.

Grandparents don't have to be smart.

They have to answer questions like "Why isn't God married?" And "How come dogs chase cats?"

When they read to us, they don't skip. They don't mind if we ask for the same story over again.

Everybody should try to have a grandmother, especially if you don't have television, because they are the only grown ups who like to spend time with us.

They know we should have snack time before bedtime and they say prayers with us every time, and kiss us when we've acted bad.

I am privileged to have 15 beautiful grand kids and each one has their own wonderful personality. If you haven't spent much time with some of them, now is a good time to phone or write them and tell them how much you love them. Of coarse you know you love them, but it is always extra special for them to hear you say it. Don't delay.

I am so lucky because even at my age I can say I have a new 17 year old daughter who calls me papa. We answered God's call to become a foster parent and He rewarded my wife and I by giving us a young daughter. How can I ever feel old?

CLOSING PRAYER

I've always been fascinated by Indian Lore and wrote a poem that is more like a prayer.

GREAT WHITE SPIRIT

O Great White Spirit of sun and trees
Of rippling waters and summer breeze,
We bow our head in great appreciation
For Your mighty works, Your creation.
We watch Your sun set at close of day,
And Your moon rise over yonder bay.
You spread Your hands and the lake is still,
All creation bows to Your will.

O Great Spirit of sea and sky,
Make straight our pathways until we
die.
Guide our moccasins on sacred ground,
Sharpen our ears to hear Your sound.
As the great eagle glides through space
And we gaze upward, help us to see Your
face.

O Great Spirit of moon and stars,
We stand in awe at how great You are,
And as we stand alone by the mighty pine
And the last arrow is gone from the

quiver of time
And no more on this earth will we roam,
Open Your arms and welcome us home.

God Bless all of you and may the rest of your life be filled with happiness and may your heart be filled with the spirit of love for you cannot really exist without it. But I know you already have an abundance of love to give. Never hesitate to give a person a smile, it might be just what he needed to restore his faith in the human race.

Never let the sun set on your anger, be a peacemaker. Let the spark of love start with you and help spread it all around. Smile at your enemies, it will drive them crazy.

Remember the three keys to heaven are:

1- Always try to do what is right.
2- Love tenderly
3- Walk humbly with God.